© 2024 by FAISAL JAMIL. All rights reserved.

Title: "The Inflation Tide: Navigating the Global Economic Impact"

This book, along with its contents encompassing text, illustrations, images, diagrams, and other creative elements, is the exclusive property of FAISAL JAMIL and is safeguarded by copyright law.

FAISAL JAMIL asserts full ownership and retains all rights to this book. No part of this publication may be reproduced, distributed, or transmitted in any form or by any means, such as photocopying, recording, or electronic methods, without prior written consent from the copyright holder. Brief quotations in critical reviews and certain noncommercial uses permitted by copyright law are exceptions.

This copyright notice applies to all editions, formats, and translations of the book, whether in print, digital, or any other medium or technology existing now or developed in the future. Unauthorized use or infringement may result in legal action and pursuit of remedies under applicable copyright laws.

While efforts have been made to ensure accuracy and reliability, FAISAL JAMIL does not guarantee the completeness or suitability of the information. Readers are responsible for evaluating and using the content judiciously.

FAISAL JAMIL reserves the right to make changes, updates, or corrections to the book without prior notice. Inclusion of third-party materials or references does not imply endorsement or affiliation unless used under fair use principles or with proper permissions and attributions.

For permissions, inquiries, or requests regarding the book's use, please contact FAISAL JAMIL through official channels listed on their Amazon author page or provided email address.

This comprehensive copyright notice serves to protect FAISAL JAMIL'S intellectual property rights, maintain content control, and inform users about associated restrictions and permissions.

Warm regards,

FAISAL JAMIL

I Always Give's Free Copies Need Your Feedback And Reviews Keeps In Touch!

http://www.amazon.com/author/faisal.jamil

Email: faisaljamilauthor@gmail.com

About the author

Certainly! Faisal Jamil is a multifaceted individual with a diverse set of skills and experiences. With a strong foundation in computer knowledge since childhood, he has developed a deep understanding of technology that informs his work as a content writer. Faisal also possesses digital skills, which further enhance his abilities in various digital platforms and technologies.

Beyond his professional endeavors, Faisal Jamil has also excelled in the martial arts, particularly Shotokan Karate, where he achieved the prestigious rank of first Dan black belt. This achievement speaks to his dedication, discipline, and commitment to personal growth and mastery.

In his professional life, Faisal Jamil has carved out a successful career in sales management within the Fast Moving Consumer Goods (FMCG) sector. His roles in various FMCG companies have honed his skills in strategic planning, team leadership, and business development. Faisal's ability to drive sales and achieve targets has been instrumental in his career progression, showcasing his talent for identifying opportunities and delivering results.

Faisal Jamil is also deeply interested in business investment strategies, planning, and execution. His understanding of these areas has been key to his success in the business world, allowing him to make informed decisions and implement effective strategies. His ability to navigate the complexities of investment planning and execution has set him apart as a strategic thinker and a valuable asset in any business endeavor.

Overall, Faisal Jamil is a dynamic individual who combines his passion for technology, martial arts, sales management, digital skills, and business investment strategies to achieve success in diverse fields. His journey is a testament to his versatility, resilience, and continuous pursuit of excellence.

Yours Sincerely

FAISAL JAMIL

I Always Give's Free Copies Need Your Feedback And Reviews Keeps In Touch!

https://www.amazon.com/author/faisal.jamil

Email: faisaljamilauthor@gmail.com

THE INFLATION TIDE
NAVIGATING THE GLOBAL ECONOMIC IMPACT

Table of Content

Preface	8
Introduction	11
Chapter 1: The Birth of Inflation	14
Chapter 2: The Mechanics of Money	19
Chapter 3: Hyperinflation: Lessons from History	26
Chapter 4: Inflation in the Developed World	35
Chapter 5: Emerging Economies and Inflation	44
Chapter 6: The Role of Central Banks	53
Chapter 7: The Global Financial Crisis and Inflation	62
Chapter 8: Inflation and Income Inequality	71
Chapter 9: The Supply Chain and Inflation	79
Chapter 10: Technology's Impact on Inflation	87
Chapter 11: Currency Wars and Competitive Devaluation	95
Chapter 12: The Energy Sector and Inflation	103
Chapter 13: Government Debt and Inflation	113
Chapter 14: Inflation Targeting: Successes and Failures	121

Chapter 15: Social and Political Consequences of Inflation	128
Chapter 16: The Future of Inflation: Predictions and Trends	136
Chapter 17: Personal Finance and Inflation	144
Chapter 18: Global Trade and Inflation	151
Chapter 19: Case Studies in Inflation Management	159
Chapter 20: Navigating the Inflation Tide: A Global Call to Action	168

Preface

Inflation is a term that evokes both concern and curiosity. It's a phenomenon that touches every corner of the global economy, influencing the prices of goods and services, the value of money, and ultimately, the quality of life for individuals across the world. Yet, despite its ubiquitous presence, inflation remains a complex and often misunderstood concept. This book, "The Inflation Tide: Navigating the Global Economic Impact," aims to demystify inflation, providing a thorough exploration of its origins, mechanics, and implications.

My interest in inflation was sparked by the myriad of ways it influences both macroeconomic stability and personal financial well-being. As an economist, I have witnessed firsthand the far-reaching effects of inflation, from eroding purchasing power to triggering economic crises. This book is the culmination of years of research, analysis, and reflection on one of the most critical aspects of economic theory and practice.

"The Inflation Tide" is structured to guide readers through a comprehensive journey of understanding. We begin with the historical roots of inflation, tracing its evolution from ancient barter systems to the complex financial instruments of today. By exploring the mechanics of money supply and the pivotal role of central banks, we lay a foundation for understanding how inflation is managed and sometimes mismanaged.

Historical case studies, such as the hyperinflation in the Weimar Republic, Zimbabwe, and Venezuela, provide stark reminders of the catastrophic potential of unchecked inflation. Conversely, the experiences of developed economies post-World War II, and the unique challenges faced by emerging markets, illustrate the diverse strategies and outcomes in managing inflation.

The book also delves into contemporary issues that intersect with inflation, such as income inequality, supply chain disruptions, and technological advancements. We examine the role of central banks, the impact of global financial crises, and the intricate dance between fiscal policy and debt management. Case studies of successful inflation management in countries like Singapore and Switzerland offer valuable insights and best practices.

In the concluding chapters, we synthesize these insights to propose a comprehensive approach for navigating inflation in the modern world. This global call to action emphasizes the need for international cooperation, innovative policies, and a proactive stance to ensure economic stability and prosperity.

"The Inflation Tide: Navigating the Global Economic Impact" is intended for a diverse audience, including policymakers, economists, students, and anyone with a keen interest in understanding the forces shaping our global economy. My hope is that this book will serve as both an informative guide and a catalyst for thoughtful discussion on one of the most pressing economic issues of our time.

I extend my gratitude to the countless individuals whose work and insights have informed this book. I am especially thankful to my colleagues, mentors, and students who have challenged and inspired me throughout this journey. It is my sincere hope that this book will contribute to a deeper understanding of inflation and help foster more effective strategies for managing it.

Thank you for joining me on this journey to unravel the complexities of inflation. Together, we can navigate the inflation tide and chart a course toward a stable and prosperous economic future.

Sincerely,

FAISAL JAMIL

INTRODUCTION

Inflation is a term that permeates daily conversations, financial news, and economic policy debates. Yet, its complexities and far-reaching impacts are often not fully understood. "The Inflation Tide: Navigating the Global Economic Impact" aims to bridge this gap by providing a comprehensive exploration of inflation, from its historical roots to its contemporary manifestations and future implications.

Inflation, simply put, is the rate at which the general level of prices for goods and services rises, eroding purchasing power. While moderate inflation is a normal part of a growing economy, high or unpredictable inflation can have detrimental effects. It can distort spending and investment decisions, erode savings, and lead to economic instability. Understanding the nuances of inflation is crucial for policymakers, businesses, and individuals alike.

This book is structured to offer a deep dive into the multifaceted nature of inflation. We begin by tracing the origins of inflation, exploring how it has evolved from ancient barter systems to modern financial markets. The first few chapters lay the groundwork by explaining the fundamental economic principles that underpin inflation, including the roles of money supply, demand, and central banking.

Through historical case studies, we examine extreme scenarios like hyperinflation in the Weimar Republic, Zimbabwe, and Venezuela. These cases illustrate the catastrophic effects of uncontrolled inflation and the societal upheaval it can cause. We also analyze how developed nations, such as the United States, Japan, and those in the Eurozone, have managed inflation in the post-World War II era, highlighting the influence of technological advancements, globalization, and policy decisions.

Emerging economies face unique inflationary pressures. We delve into the challenges and opportunities for countries like India, Brazil, and South Africa, exploring how they balance growth with inflation control. The role of central banks, such as the Federal Reserve, the European Central Bank, and the Bank of Japan, is examined in detail, showcasing their strategies and the complexities of maintaining economic stability.

The 2008 global financial crisis marked a turning point in how inflation is perceived and managed worldwide. We analyze the crisis's causes, the varied responses by different countries, and the long-term impacts on inflation. Additionally, we explore the relationship between inflation and income inequality, examining how inflation disproportionately affects different socio-economic groups and what policies can mitigate these effects.

In the interconnected global economy, the supply chain plays a critical role in inflation dynamics. We investigate how disruptions, such as those caused by the COVID-19 pandemic, impact inflation and what measures can be taken to ensure stability. Technological advancements, from e-commerce to manufacturing innovations, also significantly influence inflation, reshaping the landscape in profound ways.

Currency wars and competitive devaluation, the energy sector's role, government debt, and inflation targeting are other critical aspects covered in this book. By examining successful inflation management strategies from countries like Singapore and Switzerland, we identify best practices and lessons learned.

The concluding chapters synthesize these insights to propose a comprehensive approach to managing inflation in today's complex and interconnected world. We call for global cooperation, innovative policies, and a proactive stance to navigate the inflation tide effectively.

"The Inflation Tide: Navigating the Global Economic Impact" is designed for a wide audience, from policymakers and economists to students and curious readers. By providing a thorough understanding of inflation's intricacies and impacts, this book aims to equip readers with the knowledge needed to navigate one of the most pressing economic issues of our time.

As we embark on this journey, I invite you to delve into the intricate world of inflation, to understand its past, grapple with its present, and anticipate its future. Together, we can explore how to manage this powerful economic force, ensuring stability and prosperity for economies around the globe.

Welcome to "The Inflation Tide: Navigating the Global Economic Impact."

Chapter 1
The Birth of Inflation

Introduction

Inflation, a term that often conjures images of rising prices and eroded purchasing power, is a phenomenon with deep historical roots. Understanding its origins provides critical insights into its mechanisms and impacts on modern economies. This chapter embarks on a journey from ancient economies to contemporary financial systems, illuminating the fundamental economic principles that underpin inflation and its evolution over centuries.

Ancient Economies and the Concept of Value

The origins of inflation can be traced back to the earliest forms of trade and commerce. In ancient economies, bartering was the primary means of exchange. Goods were traded directly for other goods, and the concept of money was yet to be invented. However, as societies grew and trade networks expanded, the limitations of bartering became apparent.

The introduction of commodity money, such as cattle, grains, and precious metals, marked a significant advancement. These commodities had intrinsic value and were widely accepted in exchange for goods and services. Yet, the value of these commodities could fluctuate due to changes in supply and demand, introducing early forms of inflationary pressures. For instance, a bountiful harvest could decrease the value of grains, leading to higher prices for other goods.

The Rise of Coinage and Early Monetary Systems

The invention of coinage around the 7th century BCE in Lydia (modern-day Turkey) revolutionized economic systems. Coins made from precious metals like gold, silver, and copper became standardized units of value, facilitating trade and commerce. However, the issuance of coinage also introduced new inflationary dynamics.

Governments and rulers quickly realized that by debasing their currency—reducing the precious metal content of coins—they could produce more money to fund wars, public works, and other expenditures. This practice, known as seigniorage, often led to inflation. For example, during the Roman Empire, the denarius was gradually debased over centuries, resulting in significant inflation and economic instability.

Medieval and Renaissance Inflation

The medieval period saw the continuation of coinage systems, but inflationary pressures persisted. One notable episode was the influx of precious metals from the New World during the 16th century, which flooded European markets with gold and silver. This sudden increase in money supply, particularly in Spain, led to widespread inflation known as the "Price Revolution."

During the Renaissance, the expansion of trade and the emergence of banking systems further influenced inflationary trends. Banks began issuing paper money and promissory notes, which increased the money supply and, at times, led to inflation. The Medici Bank in Florence, for example, played a pivotal role in the financial innovations of the period, highlighting the growing complexity of monetary systems.

The Industrial Revolution and the Birth of Modern Inflation

The Industrial Revolution of the 18th and 19th centuries marked a turning point in economic history. The introduction of mechanized production, mass manufacturing, and improved transportation dramatically increased economic output. However, it also introduced new inflationary dynamics.

The expansion of credit and the creation of central banks, such as the Bank of England in 1694, transformed the financial landscape. Central banks began to play a crucial role in managing inflation through monetary policy. The ability to issue banknotes and control interest rates allowed central banks to influence the money supply and, consequently, inflation.

The Gold Standard and Inflation Control

The 19th century saw the widespread adoption of the gold standard, where currencies were directly linked to gold reserves. This system was designed to provide monetary stability and control inflation. By tying the money supply to gold reserves, governments aimed to prevent excessive inflation.

However, the gold standard was not without its challenges. Economic shocks, such as the discovery of new gold mines or changes in gold production, could still influence inflation. The gold standard also limited governments' ability to respond to economic crises, as they were constrained by their gold reserves.

The 20th Century: Wars, Crises, and Inflation

The 20th century witnessed significant inflationary episodes driven by wars, economic crises, and policy decisions. World War I and World War II had profound inflationary impacts as governments printed money to finance military expenditures. The hyperinflation in Weimar Germany during the 1920s remains one of the most extreme examples, where prices soared and the currency became virtually worthless.

The post-World War II era saw the establishment of the Bretton Woods system, where currencies were pegged to the US dollar, which was convertible to gold. This system aimed to provide global monetary stability but eventually collapsed in the 1970s, leading to the modern era of fiat currencies.

Fiat Money and Contemporary Inflation

The abandonment of the gold standard and the transition to fiat money—currencies without intrinsic value and not backed by physical commodities—marked a new chapter in the history of inflation. Central banks gained greater flexibility in managing monetary policy, but the potential for inflationary pressures remained.

Inflation became a focal point for economic policy, with central banks using tools such as interest rate adjustments, open market operations, and reserve requirements to control inflation. The 1970s oil shocks and the subsequent stagflation (a combination of inflation and stagnant economic growth) highlighted the challenges of managing inflation in a complex global economy.

Conclusion

The journey from ancient economies to modern financial systems reveals that inflation is a multifaceted phenomenon influenced by a myriad of factors, including money supply, demand, production, and policy decisions. Understanding the historical context of inflation provides valuable insights into its mechanisms and the ongoing efforts to manage it in today's interconnected world.

In the following chapters, we will explore how these historical foundations have shaped contemporary inflation dynamics and the global impact of inflation in various regions and sectors. By examining the past, we gain a deeper appreciation of the challenges and opportunities that lie ahead in navigating the inflation tide.

Chapter 2
The Mechanics of Money

Introduction

Money is the lifeblood of modern economies, facilitating trade, investment, and consumption. Understanding the mechanics of money—how it is created, circulated, and controlled—is essential to grasping the complexities of inflation. This chapter delves into the intricate workings of money supply and demand, the pivotal role of central banks, and the various monetary policy tools they employ to regulate inflation.

The Money Supply

The money supply refers to the total amount of monetary assets available in an economy at a specific time. It includes physical currency (coins and notes) and various types of deposits held in banks. Economists typically categorize the money supply into several aggregates, each representing different levels of liquidity:

M0 (Monetary Base):

The most liquid form of money, including physical currency and coins in circulation, along with reserves held by commercial banks at the central bank.

M1:

Includes M0 plus demand deposits (checking accounts) and other liquid assets that can be quickly converted to cash.

M2:

Includes M1 plus savings accounts, time deposits (such as certificates of deposit), and non-institutional money market funds.

M3:

Includes M2 plus large time deposits, institutional money market funds, and other larger liquid assets.

The control and manipulation of these aggregates are central to understanding how monetary policy impacts inflation.

The Demand for Money

The demand for money refers to the desire of households, businesses, and governments to hold money rather than invest it in other assets. Several factors influence the demand for money:

Transactions Motive:

The need for money to conduct everyday transactions. This demand increases with higher income and consumption levels.

Precautionary Motive:

The desire to hold money for unexpected expenses or emergencies.

Speculative Motive:

The preference to hold money instead of other assets due to expectations of future changes in interest rates or asset prices.

Central Banks: The Guardians of Monetary Stability

Central banks, such as the Federal Reserve in the United States, the European Central Bank, and the Bank of Japan, play a crucial role in regulating the money supply and ensuring monetary stability. They are responsible for implementing monetary policy, which aims to achieve macroeconomic objectives such as controlling inflation, managing employment levels, and stabilizing the financial system.

Monetary Policy Tools

Central banks have a range of tools at their disposal to influence the money supply and demand, thereby regulating inflation. The primary tools include:

Interest Rates

Policy Rates:

Central banks set key policy interest rates, such as the federal funds rate in the United States, which influence other interest rates in the economy. By raising or lowering these rates, central banks can make borrowing more or less expensive, thereby influencing spending and investment.

Transmission Mechanism:

Changes in policy rates affect consumer and business loans, mortgages, and savings rates, which in turn impact aggregate demand and inflation. Lower interest rates typically stimulate borrowing and spending, leading to higher inflation, while higher rates tend to have the opposite effect.

Reserve Requirements

Definition:

Reserve requirements refer to the minimum amount of reserves that commercial banks must hold against their deposits. These reserves are typically held at the central bank.

Impact on Money Supply:

By adjusting reserve requirements, central banks can influence the amount of money banks can lend. Lowering reserve requirements increases the money supply by allowing banks to lend more, while raising them restricts lending and reduces the money supply.

Open Market Operations (OMOs)

Definition:

OMOs involve the buying and selling of government securities in the open market to regulate the money supply.

Mechanism:

When a central bank buys government securities, it injects liquidity into the banking system, increasing the money supply and lowering interest rates. Conversely, selling securities withdraws liquidity, reducing the money supply and raising interest rates.

Quantitative Easing (QE)

Definition:

QE is an unconventional monetary policy tool used by central banks to stimulate the economy when conventional tools, like lowering interest rates, are insufficient.

Mechanism:

QE involves the large-scale purchase of financial assets, such as government bonds and mortgage-backed securities, to increase the money supply and lower long-term interest rates. This encourages borrowing and investment, aiming to boost economic activity and counter deflationary pressures.

Discount Rate

Definition:

The discount rate is the interest rate charged by central banks on loans to commercial banks.

Impact:

By adjusting the discount rate, central banks can influence the cost of borrowing for commercial banks. A lower discount rate encourages banks to borrow more and lend more, increasing the money supply, while a higher rate has the opposite effect.

Inflation Targeting and Central Bank Independence

Many central banks adopt an inflation targeting framework, setting explicit inflation targets to anchor expectations and guide monetary policy. For instance, the Federal Reserve aims for a 2% inflation rate over the long run. By committing to an inflation target, central banks can build credibility and manage public expectations, making it easier to control actual inflation.

Central bank independence is another critical aspect of effective monetary policy. When central banks operate free from political interference, they can make decisions based on economic conditions rather than political pressures, enhancing their ability to maintain price stability.

The Global Perspective

The role and effectiveness of central banks vary across countries, influenced by different economic structures, levels of development, and institutional frameworks. In emerging markets, central banks often face additional challenges, such as higher volatility in capital flows and less developed financial systems. Consequently, their approaches to managing inflation may differ from those in advanced economies.

Conclusion

The mechanics of money involve a complex interplay between supply and demand, influenced by central banks' actions and broader economic conditions. By understanding the tools and strategies used by central banks to regulate inflation, we gain a clearer picture of how monetary policy shapes economic outcomes.

In subsequent chapters, we will explore the impact of inflation across various sectors and regions, examining case studies and real-world examples to illustrate the far-reaching effects of inflation. Through this comprehensive analysis, we aim to equip readers with a deeper understanding of one of the most critical aspects of economic management.

Chapter 3
Hyperinflation
Lessons from History

Introduction

Hyperinflation is an economic nightmare characterized by runaway inflation rates, where prices increase rapidly and uncontrollably. This chapter examines historical instances of hyperinflation, focusing on the Weimar Republic, Zimbabwe, and Venezuela. By analyzing these case studies, we aim to understand the triggers, effects, and societal impacts of hyperinflation, and explore how countries can recover from such extreme scenarios.

Understanding Hyperinflation

Hyperinflation occurs when the inflation rate exceeds 50% per month, leading to a rapid erosion of a currency's value. Unlike regular inflation, which is typically a gradual process, hyperinflation is swift and devastating, often rendering money virtually worthless. The causes of hyperinflation are multifaceted, involving complex interactions between economic, political, and social factors.

The Weimar Republic (Germany, 1921-1923)

Background:

Post-World War I Economic Conditions:

The Treaty of Versailles imposed heavy reparations on Germany, straining its already weakened economy. The government resorted to printing money to pay these reparations and other debts, significantly increasing the money supply.

Political Instability:

Frequent changes in government, political unrest, and strikes exacerbated the economic turmoil.

Causes:

Excessive Money Printing:

To meet its financial obligations, the German government printed vast amounts of paper money, leading to a dramatic increase in the money supply.

Loss of Confidence:

As prices began to rise, public confidence in the currency diminished, prompting people to spend money quickly before it lost more value, further accelerating inflation.

Effects:

Economic Devastation:

The value of the German mark plummeted, wiping out savings and making everyday transactions increasingly difficult. At the peak of hyperinflation, prices doubled every few days.

Social Impact:

The middle class was particularly hard hit, as their savings became worthless. This economic hardship led to widespread social unrest and contributed to the rise of extremist political movements, including the Nazi Party.

Recovery:

Currency Reform:

In 1923, the introduction of the Rentenmark, a new currency backed by land and industrial assets, helped stabilize the economy. The Rentenmark was eventually replaced by the Reichsmark, solidifying the recovery.

International Assistance:

The Dawes Plan of 1924 restructured Germany's reparations payments and brought in foreign loans, aiding economic stabilization.

Zimbabwe (2000s)

Background:

Economic Mismanagement:

Zimbabwe's economy began to deteriorate in the late 1990s due to land reforms that disrupted agricultural production, corruption, and mismanagement of public funds.

Political Instability:

President Robert Mugabe's government faced increasing domestic and international criticism, leading to political instability.

Causes:

Land Reforms:

The seizure of white-owned commercial farms led to a collapse in agricultural output, a key pillar of the economy.

Money Printing:

To finance a growing fiscal deficit and maintain political power, the government printed vast amounts of money, leading to hyperinflation.

Effects:

Currency Collapse:

By 2008, Zimbabwe's inflation rate reached an astronomical 79.6 billion percent month-on-month. The Zimbabwean dollar became worthless, and basic goods became unaffordable.

Humanitarian Crisis:

The hyperinflation crisis led to widespread poverty, unemployment, and emigration. Public services, including healthcare and education, collapsed.

Recovery:

Dollarization:

In 2009, Zimbabwe abandoned its currency in favor of the US dollar and other foreign currencies, which helped stabilize the economy.

Economic Reforms:

Efforts to rebuild the economy included improving fiscal discipline and re-engaging with international financial institutions for assistance and investment.

Venezuela (2010s-2020s)

Background:

Economic Policies:

Venezuela's economy, heavily reliant on oil exports, suffered from declining oil prices in the 2010s. Government policies, including price controls and extensive social spending, strained public finances.

Political Instability:

The country faced significant political turmoil, with President Nicolás Maduro's government becoming increasingly authoritarian and isolated internationally.

Causes:

Decline in Oil Revenue:

Falling oil prices drastically reduced government revenue, leading to budget deficits.

Money Printing:

The government financed deficits by printing money, leading to hyperinflation as the money supply ballooned.

Economic Controls:

Price controls and foreign exchange controls created black markets and further distorted the economy.

Effects:

Hyperinflation:

By 2018, Venezuela's inflation rate had reached 1.7 million percent. The bolívar became virtually worthless, and people struggled to afford basic necessities.

Mass Emigration:

Millions of Venezuelans fled the country to escape economic hardship, creating a regional humanitarian crisis.

Public Services Collapse:

Healthcare, education, and public infrastructure deteriorated severely, exacerbating the suffering of the population.

Recovery:

Economic Measures:

The government introduced new currency denominations and attempted to stabilize the economy through price liberalization and engaging with international creditors.

International Aid:

Efforts to secure international assistance and investment have been crucial in providing immediate relief and fostering longer-term recovery.

Common Triggers of Hyperinflation

Through these case studies, several common triggers of hyperinflation emerge:

Excessive Money Printing:

Governments resort to printing money to finance deficits, leading to an oversupply of currency.

Loss of Confidence:

Public trust in the currency erodes, prompting rapid spending and hoarding of real assets.

Political Instability:

Political turmoil and weak governance exacerbate economic mismanagement.

Economic Shocks:

External shocks, such as declining commodity prices or war, can disrupt economic stability and trigger hyperinflation.

Societal Impact of Hyperinflation

Hyperinflation wreaks havoc on societies, with profound and far-reaching consequences:

Wealth Erosion:

Savings and fixed incomes are wiped out, disproportionately affecting the middle class and vulnerable populations.

Social Unrest:

Economic hardship leads to social unrest, protests, and, in some cases, the rise of extremist political movements.

Humanitarian Crises:

Basic goods become unaffordable, leading to widespread poverty, malnutrition, and deteriorating public services.

Strategies for Recovery

Recovering from hyperinflation is challenging but achievable through a combination of measures:

Currency Stabilization:

Introducing a stable and credible currency, often backed by real assets or foreign reserves, is crucial.

Fiscal Discipline:

Governments must implement fiscal reforms to control deficits and reduce reliance on money printing.

International Assistance:

Engaging with international financial institutions and securing foreign aid can provide the necessary support for recovery.

Economic Reforms:

Structural reforms, such as liberalizing markets, improving governance, and fostering economic diversification, are essential for long-term stability.

Conclusion

Hyperinflation is a devastating economic phenomenon with profound societal impacts. By examining historical case studies, we gain valuable insights into the triggers, effects, and recovery strategies associated with hyperinflation. These lessons underscore the importance of sound economic management, political stability, and international cooperation in preventing and mitigating the impacts of hyperinflation.

In the following chapters, we will explore the broader implications of inflation, including its impact on income inequality, global trade, and personal finance, providing a comprehensive understanding of this complex economic issue.

Chapter 4
Inflation in the Developed World

Introduction

In the post-World War II era, developed nations have faced various inflationary pressures and implemented diverse strategies to manage inflation. This chapter examines how the United States, Japan, and the Eurozone have tackled inflation through economic policies, technological advancements, and globalization. We explore the unique challenges and successes these regions have experienced in maintaining price stability and promoting economic growth.

The United States: From Post-War Boom to Modern Challenges

Post-World War II Economic Boom:

Economic Expansion:

The post-war period saw rapid economic growth in the United States, driven by industrial production, consumer spending, and government investment.

Moderate Inflation:

Initially, the U.S. experienced moderate inflation as demand for goods and services surged, but this was largely managed through effective monetary policies.

The 1970s Stagflation:

Oil Shocks:

The oil crises of 1973 and 1979 led to skyrocketing energy prices, triggering inflationary pressures.

Stagflation:

The U.S. faced stagflation, a combination of high inflation and stagnant economic growth, challenging conventional economic theories and policies.

Monetary Policy Response:

The Federal Reserve, under Chairman Paul Volcker, implemented aggressive interest rate hikes to curb inflation, leading to a severe but necessary economic recession.

Technological Advancements and Productivity Gains:

Information Technology Revolution:

The late 20th and early 21st centuries saw significant technological advancements, particularly in information technology, which boosted productivity and helped moderate inflation.

Global Supply Chains:

The globalization of supply chains and the offshoring of manufacturing to lower-cost countries helped keep production costs down, contributing to low inflation.

The Great Recession and Aftermath:

2008 Financial Crisis:

The collapse of the housing market and subsequent financial crisis led to deflationary pressures as demand plummeted.

Quantitative Easing:

The Federal Reserve implemented unconventional monetary policies, including quantitative easing (QE), to stimulate the economy and prevent deflation.

Post-Crisis Inflation Control:

Despite fears of hyperinflation due to expansive monetary policy, inflation remained subdued, highlighting the complex interplay between monetary policy, economic conditions, and inflation expectations.

Japan: Battling Deflation and Stagnation

The Bubble Economy and Its Collapse:

1980s Asset Bubble:

Japan experienced a massive asset bubble in real estate and stock markets during the 1980s, fueled by speculative investment and easy credit.

Bubble Burst:

The bubble burst in the early 1990s, leading to a prolonged period of economic stagnation and deflation, known as the "Lost Decade."

Deflationary Spiral:

Price Declines:

Persistent deflation, characterized by falling prices, reduced consumer spending and investment, further exacerbating economic stagnation.

Monetary Policy Challenges:

The Bank of Japan (BOJ) struggled to combat deflation, with conventional monetary tools proving ineffective in stimulating demand.

Abenomics and Unconventional Policies:

Three Arrows Strategy:

In 2012, Prime Minister Shinzo Abe introduced "Abenomics," a three-pronged strategy focusing on aggressive monetary easing, fiscal stimulus, and structural reforms.

Quantitative and Qualitative Easing (QQE):

The BOJ implemented QQE, purchasing large quantities of government bonds and other assets to inject liquidity into the economy and encourage inflation.

Mixed Results:

While Abenomics achieved some success in stabilizing prices and boosting economic growth, deflationary pressures persisted, underscoring the difficulty of overcoming entrenched deflation.

The Eurozone: A Unified Approach to Inflation

Formation of the Eurozone:

Economic and Monetary Union (EMU):

The creation of the Eurozone in 1999 unified the monetary policy of member states under the European Central Bank (ECB).

Price Stability Mandate:

The ECB's primary mandate is to maintain price stability, targeting an inflation rate of close to but below 2%.

Inflation Divergence and Policy Challenges:

Diverse Economies:

The Eurozone comprises diverse economies with varying inflation rates and economic conditions, complicating the ECB's task of implementing a one-size-fits-all monetary policy.

Sovereign Debt Crisis:

The 2010 European sovereign debt crisis highlighted the challenges of managing inflation and economic stability in a currency union without a unified fiscal policy.

Unconventional Monetary Policies:

Negative Interest Rates:

The ECB introduced negative interest rates to encourage borrowing and spending, countering deflationary pressures.

Quantitative Easing:

Like the Federal Reserve and BOJ, the ECB implemented QE, purchasing government and corporate bonds to inject liquidity into the economy.

Inflation Targeting:

Despite these efforts, achieving the ECB's inflation target has been challenging, with inflation remaining stubbornly low in the years following the financial crisis.

The Role of Technological Advancements

Technological advancements have played a significant role in shaping inflation dynamics in developed economies. Key areas of impact include:

Productivity Gains:

Automation and Efficiency:

Advances in automation, artificial intelligence, and information technology have boosted productivity, allowing for more efficient production processes and cost reductions.

Moderating Inflation:

Increased productivity helps moderate inflation by reducing production costs and enabling businesses to meet rising demand without raising prices significantly.

Globalization and Supply Chains:

Offshoring and Outsourcing:

The globalization of supply chains and the offshoring of manufacturing to countries with lower labor costs have kept production costs down, contributing to lower inflation in developed economies.

Technological Integration:

Improved logistics, communication, and information technology have enhanced the efficiency of global supply chains, further moderating inflationary pressures.

E-Commerce and Competition:

Price Transparency:

The rise of e-commerce platforms has increased price transparency and competition, putting downward pressure on prices.

Consumer Choice:

Online shopping provides consumers with more choices and the ability to compare prices easily, discouraging price increases.

Economic Policies and Inflation Management

Economic policies have been pivotal in managing inflation in developed economies. Key strategies include:

Monetary Policy:

Interest Rate Adjustments:

Central banks use interest rate adjustments to influence borrowing, spending, and investment, thereby controlling inflation.

Forward Guidance:

Communicating future policy intentions helps manage inflation expectations and provides stability to financial markets.

Fiscal Policy:

Government Spending and Taxation:

Fiscal policy, through government spending and taxation, can influence aggregate demand and inflation. During economic downturns, fiscal stimulus can boost demand and counter deflationary pressures.

Debt Management:

Effective debt management ensures that government borrowing does not lead to excessive inflation or crowd out private investment.

Structural Reforms:

Labor Market Flexibility:

Reforms to increase labor market flexibility, enhance skills, and improve employment opportunities can help moderate wage inflation and support economic growth.

Regulatory Reforms:

Reducing regulatory burdens and promoting competition can lower costs and enhance productivity, contributing to price stability.

Conclusion

The post-World War II era has seen developed nations navigate a complex landscape of inflationary pressures through a combination of economic policies, technological advancements, and globalization. The experiences of the United States, Japan, and the Eurozone illustrate the diverse challenges and strategies in managing inflation.

In the following chapters, we will explore the impact of inflation in emerging economies, the role of central banks, and the relationship between inflation and income inequality, providing a comprehensive understanding of how inflation shapes global economic dynamics.

Chapter 5
Emerging Economies and Inflation

Introduction

Emerging economies, characterized by rapid growth and industrialization, face unique inflationary pressures compared to developed nations. This chapter explores the challenges and opportunities in managing inflation in countries like India, Brazil, and South Africa. We examine the factors contributing to inflation in these economies, the strategies employed to balance growth with inflation control, and the lessons learned from their experiences.

The Nature of Inflation in Emerging Economies

Emerging markets often experience higher and more volatile inflation rates due to various factors such as economic growth patterns, structural issues, and external vulnerabilities. Key characteristics include:

High Growth Rates:

Rapid economic expansion can lead to demand-pull inflation, where increased demand outstrips supply.

Structural Constraints:

Infrastructural deficits, supply chain inefficiencies, and limited production capacities contribute to cost-push inflation.

External Shocks:

Emerging economies are more susceptible to external shocks, such as commodity price fluctuations and changes in global financial conditions, impacting inflation.

India: Balancing Growth and Inflation

Economic Context:

High Growth Potential:

India is one of the fastest-growing major economies, with significant contributions from sectors like services, manufacturing, and agriculture.

Structural Challenges:

Despite rapid growth, India faces structural issues such as inadequate infrastructure, supply chain inefficiencies, and a large informal economy.

Inflation Dynamics:

Food Prices:

Food inflation is a major component of overall inflation due to the significant share of food in the consumption basket and supply chain bottlenecks.

Fiscal Deficits:

High fiscal deficits and public debt levels contribute to inflationary pressures by increasing money supply and aggregate demand.

Monetary Policy:

The Reserve Bank of India (RBI) uses interest rates and other monetary tools to manage inflation. However, balancing inflation control with the need for economic growth remains a challenge.

Policy Measures:

Inflation Targeting:

In 2016, India adopted a formal inflation targeting framework, setting a target range of 2-6% to anchor inflation expectations and enhance policy credibility.

Supply-Side Reforms:

Efforts to improve infrastructure, streamline supply chains, and enhance agricultural productivity aim to address structural bottlenecks and reduce cost-push inflation.

Monetary Policy Adjustments:

The RBI adjusts interest rates based on inflation trends and economic conditions, balancing the dual objectives of price stability and growth.

Brazil: Coping with Economic Volatility

Economic Context:

Commodity Dependence:

Brazil's economy is heavily reliant on commodities like oil, iron ore, and agricultural products, making it vulnerable to global price fluctuations.

Political Instability:

Frequent political changes and corruption scandals have led to economic uncertainty and volatility.

Inflation Dynamics:

Commodity Prices:

Fluctuations in global commodity prices have a significant impact on Brazil's inflation, given the economy's reliance on commodity exports.

Exchange Rate Volatility:

Depreciation of the Brazilian real increases the cost of imported goods, contributing to inflation.

Fiscal Policies:

Government spending and fiscal deficits, particularly during periods of political instability, add to inflationary pressures.

Policy Measures:

Inflation Targeting:

The Central Bank of Brazil adopts an inflation targeting regime, aiming to keep inflation within a specified range to maintain price stability and economic predictability.

Monetary Policy:

Interest rate adjustments are the primary tool for controlling inflation, with the central bank frequently intervening to manage inflation expectations and stabilize the currency.

Structural Reforms:

Efforts to diversify the economy, improve fiscal discipline, and reduce dependence on commodities are critical for long-term inflation control.

South Africa: Navigating Structural Constraints

Economic Context:

Structural Challenges:

South Africa faces significant structural issues, including high unemployment, income inequality, and inadequate infrastructure.

Commodity Exports:

The economy is heavily reliant on mining and commodity exports, exposing it to global market fluctuations.

Inflation Dynamics:

Supply Constraints:

Structural issues such as power shortages and infrastructural deficits contribute to cost-push inflation.

Exchange Rate Movements:

The South African rand's volatility affects import prices, contributing to inflation.

Wage Pressures:

High unemployment and labor strikes often lead to wage increases, adding to inflationary pressures.

Policy Measures:

Inflation Targeting:

The South African Reserve Bank (SARB) employs an inflation targeting framework, with a target range of 3-6% to anchor inflation expectations.

Monetary Policy:

The SARB uses interest rate adjustments and other monetary tools to manage inflation, balancing the need for price stability with economic growth.

Structural Reforms:

Policies aimed at improving infrastructure, enhancing energy supply, and promoting economic diversification are crucial for addressing structural inflationary pressures.

Common Challenges and Strategies in Emerging Economies

Balancing Growth and Inflation:

Economic Growth:

Rapid growth in emerging economies can lead to increased demand and inflationary pressures. Policymakers must balance stimulating growth with maintaining price stability.

Monetary Policy:

Central banks in emerging economies often face the challenge of using monetary policy to control inflation without stifling growth. Interest rate adjustments must be carefully calibrated to manage inflation expectations while supporting economic activity.

Structural Reforms:

Infrastructure Development:

Improving infrastructure, such as transportation, energy supply, and logistics, can reduce supply-side constraints and lower production costs, helping to control inflation.

Enhancing Productivity:

Investments in technology, education, and skills development can boost productivity, reducing cost-push inflation and supporting sustainable growth.

Managing External Shocks:

Commodity Price Volatility:

Emerging economies reliant on commodity exports must develop strategies to manage the impact of global price fluctuations on inflation. Diversifying the economy and building foreign exchange reserves can help mitigate these risks.

Exchange Rate Stability:

Maintaining a stable exchange rate is crucial for controlling imported inflation. Central banks may use foreign exchange interventions and monetary policy adjustments to stabilize the currency.

Fiscal Discipline:

Controlling Deficits:

High fiscal deficits and public debt levels contribute to inflationary pressures. Implementing fiscal discipline through prudent government spending and revenue generation is essential for long-term price stability.

Structural Adjustments:

Structural fiscal reforms, such as reducing subsidies, broadening the tax base, and improving public financial management, can help control inflation.

Lessons Learned and Future Directions

Emerging economies provide valuable lessons in managing inflation amidst rapid growth and structural challenges:

Importance of Policy Credibility:

Establishing credible monetary and fiscal policies is essential for managing inflation expectations and maintaining economic stability. Transparent communication and consistent policy implementation build public and investor confidence.

Role of Central Banks:

Independent and empowered central banks play a crucial role in controlling inflation. Effective monetary policy frameworks, such as inflation targeting, provide a clear anchor for inflation expectations and enhance policy effectiveness.

Need for Structural Reforms:

Addressing structural constraints through targeted reforms is vital for long-term inflation control. Investments in infrastructure, education, and technology, along with efforts to diversify the economy, reduce inflationary pressures and support sustainable growth.

Resilience to External Shocks:

Developing resilience to external shocks, such as commodity price fluctuations and global financial volatility, is critical for maintaining price stability. Building foreign exchange reserves, diversifying exports, and enhancing economic flexibility are key strategies.

Conclusion

Emerging economies face unique inflationary challenges due to rapid growth, structural constraints, and external vulnerabilities. Countries like India, Brazil, and South Africa provide valuable insights into the complexities of managing inflation while promoting economic development. By balancing growth with inflation control, implementing structural reforms, and building resilience to external shocks, these economies can achieve sustainable and inclusive growth.

In the following chapters, we will delve into the role of central banks in managing inflation, the relationship between inflation and income inequality, and the impact of inflation on global trade, providing a comprehensive understanding of inflation's multifaceted nature in the global economy.

Chapter 6
The Role of Central Banks

Introduction

Central banks play a crucial role in managing inflation and ensuring economic stability. Institutions like the Federal Reserve (Fed), the European Central Bank (ECB), and the Bank of Japan (BOJ) are at the forefront of formulating and implementing monetary policies aimed at controlling inflation. This chapter explores the strategies employed by these central banks, examines their successes and failures, and discusses their impact on economic stability.

The Functions of Central Banks

Central banks have several key functions that directly or indirectly influence inflation and economic stability:

Monetary Policy Formulation and Implementation:

Interest Rates: Central banks set benchmark interest rates, which influence borrowing and lending rates throughout the economy. Lower rates generally stimulate economic activity but can also lead to higher inflation, while higher rates tend to slow down the economy and curb inflation.

Open Market Operations: By buying or selling government securities, central banks control the money supply and liquidity in the financial system.

Reserve Requirements: Adjusting the reserve requirements for commercial banks influences the amount of money they can lend, affecting overall economic activity and inflation.

Inflation Targeting:

Central banks often set explicit inflation targets to anchor expectations and provide a clear framework for monetary policy. Inflation targeting helps stabilize prices and provides transparency and predictability to financial markets.

Financial Stability:

Central banks oversee the banking system to ensure its stability and soundness. By acting as a lender of last resort during financial crises, they help maintain confidence in the financial system and prevent systemic risks.

Foreign Exchange Management:

In some cases, central banks intervene in foreign exchange markets to stabilize their currency, impacting inflation through the prices of imported goods and services.

The Federal Reserve (Fed): Managing U.S. Inflation

Monetary Policy Tools:

Federal Funds Rate:

The Fed's primary tool for managing inflation is the federal funds rate, the interest rate at which banks lend to each other overnight. Changes in this rate influence other interest rates, including those for mortgages, credit cards, and business loans.

Quantitative Easing (QE):

During economic crises, such as the 2008 financial crisis and the COVID-19 pandemic, the Fed employed QE by purchasing large quantities of government and mortgage-backed securities to inject liquidity into the economy and lower long-term interest rates.

Forward Guidance:

The Fed uses forward guidance to communicate its future policy intentions, influencing market expectations and economic decisions.

Successes:

Post-2008 Recovery:

The Fed's aggressive use of QE and low interest rates helped stabilize financial markets and support economic recovery following the 2008 financial crisis.

Pandemic Response:

During the COVID-19 pandemic, the Fed's swift actions, including lowering interest rates to near zero and implementing massive QE programs, helped cushion the economic impact and support recovery.

Failures:

2000s Housing Bubble:

Critics argue that the Fed's low interest rates in the early 2000s contributed to the housing bubble and subsequent financial crisis.

Inflation Surge:

Recently, the Fed has faced criticism for underestimating inflationary pressures, leading to a delayed response in raising interest rates as inflation surged post-pandemic.

The European Central Bank (ECB): Navigating a Complex Monetary Union

Monetary Policy Tools:

Main Refinancing Operations (MRO):

The ECB uses MROs to provide liquidity to the banking system, setting the benchmark interest rate for the Eurozone.

Negative Interest Rates:

In an effort to combat low inflation and stimulate economic activity, the ECB has implemented negative interest rates, charging banks for holding excess reserves.

Asset Purchase Program (APP):

Similar to the Fed's QE, the ECB's APP involves purchasing government and corporate bonds to inject liquidity and lower borrowing costs.

Successes:

Eurozone Stability:

The ECB's policies have helped stabilize the Eurozone economy during various crises, including the sovereign debt crisis and the COVID-19 pandemic.

Low Inflation Environment:

The ECB has maintained low and stable inflation for most of its existence, contributing to economic stability in the Eurozone.

Failures:

Sovereign Debt Crisis:

The ECB's initial response to the European sovereign debt crisis was criticized for being slow and insufficient, exacerbating economic distress in several member countries.

Persistently Low Inflation:

Despite extensive monetary easing, the ECB has struggled to achieve its inflation target, with inflation remaining below target for extended periods.

The Bank of Japan (BOJ): Combatting Deflation

Monetary Policy Tools:

Short-Term Policy Rate:

The BOJ sets the short-term policy rate to influence overall economic activity and inflation.

Quantitative and Qualitative Easing (QQE):

The BOJ's QQE program involves purchasing government bonds and other assets, aiming to increase the money supply and achieve its inflation target.

Yield Curve Control (YCC):

Under YCC, the BOJ targets specific yields on government bonds, aiming to control long-term interest rates and support economic activity.

Successes:

Deflation Mitigation:

The BOJ's aggressive monetary policies have helped mitigate deflationary pressures and stabilize the economy.

Economic Support:

During the COVID-19 pandemic, the BOJ's swift actions, including increased asset purchases and liquidity support, helped cushion the economic impact and support recovery.

Failures:

Entrenched Deflation:

Despite extensive monetary easing, the BOJ has struggled to achieve its 2% inflation target, with deflationary pressures persisting for decades.

Bank Profitability:

Negative interest rates and extensive QE have put pressure on the profitability of Japanese banks, potentially undermining financial stability in the long term.

Comparative Analysis: Strategies and Outcomes

Inflation Targeting:

Fed:

The Fed's flexible inflation targeting allows it to balance price stability with other economic objectives, such as full employment. This dual mandate provides flexibility but can complicate policy decisions.

ECB:

The ECB's primary mandate is price stability, with a strict inflation target of close to but below 2%. This singular focus helps anchor inflation expectations but can limit policy responses to other economic challenges.

BOJ:

The BOJ's struggle with deflation has led to a focus on achieving positive inflation, with an official target of 2%. Despite innovative policies, achieving this target has proven difficult.

Monetary Policy Innovation:

Fed:

The Fed's use of QE and forward guidance has been instrumental in managing economic crises and stabilizing inflation expectations.

ECB:

The ECB's adoption of negative interest rates and asset purchases represents significant innovation in the face of low inflation and economic stagnation.

BOJ:

The BOJ's QQE and YCC policies highlight its willingness to experiment with unconventional tools to combat deflation and stimulate growth.

Challenges and Criticisms:

Fed:

Critics argue that the Fed's policies contributed to asset bubbles and financial instability. Additionally, recent challenges in managing post-pandemic inflation highlight the difficulties of balancing multiple mandates.

ECB:

The ECB's slow response to the sovereign debt crisis and persistent low inflation have been points of criticism. The complexities of managing a diverse monetary union add to its challenges.

BOJ:

The BOJ's prolonged struggle with deflation and the adverse effects of negative interest rates on bank profitability underscore the challenges of managing an entrenched low-inflation environment.

Conclusion

Central banks are pivotal in managing inflation and ensuring economic stability. The experiences of the Federal Reserve, the European Central Bank, and the Bank of Japan illustrate the diverse strategies, successes, and challenges in achieving these goals. Through innovative policies and a commitment to price stability, central banks strive to navigate complex economic landscapes and support sustainable growth.

In the following chapters, we will explore the relationship between inflation and income inequality, the impact of inflation on global trade, and the broader social and economic consequences of inflation, providing a comprehensive understanding of its multifaceted nature in the global economy.

Chapter 7
The Global Financial Crisis and Inflation

Introduction

The 2008 Global Financial Crisis (GFC) was a watershed event with far-reaching implications for economies worldwide. This chapter explores the origins of the crisis, the immediate and long-term impacts on inflation, and the various responses by countries to manage these effects. By examining the interplay between the crisis and inflation, we gain insights into how financial shocks influence price stability and economic policies.

Causes of the Global Financial Crisis

Housing Market Collapse:

Subprime Mortgage Crisis:

The crisis originated in the U.S. housing market, where an increase in subprime mortgage lending led to a housing bubble. When housing prices began to decline, borrowers defaulted on their loans, causing significant losses for financial institutions.

Securitization and Derivatives:

The widespread practice of securitizing mortgages into mortgage-backed securities (MBS) and collateralized debt obligations (CDOs) spread the risk throughout the global financial system. When defaults rose, the value of these securities plummeted, leading to massive losses.

Financial Sector Weaknesses:

Leverage and Risk-Taking:

Financial institutions had high leverage ratios, amplifying their exposure to the housing market downturn. Excessive risk-taking, often driven by inadequate regulatory oversight, further exacerbated the crisis.

Interconnectedness:

The global financial system's interconnected nature meant that problems in the U.S. quickly spread to other countries. Banks and investors worldwide were exposed to U.S. mortgage-backed assets, leading to a domino effect of financial distress.

Regulatory Failures:

Inadequate Oversight:

Regulatory bodies failed to keep pace with financial innovation and the increasing complexity of financial products. This lack of oversight allowed risky lending practices to proliferate.

Moral Hazard:

Policies encouraging home ownership and the belief that certain institutions were "too big to fail" contributed to moral hazard, where entities took on excessive risk under the assumption of government bailouts if things went wrong.

Responses to the Crisis

Immediate Monetary Policy Responses:

Interest Rate Cuts:

Central banks worldwide, including the Federal Reserve, the European Central Bank, and the Bank of Japan, slashed interest rates to near zero to stimulate economic activity and prevent deflation.

Quantitative Easing (QE):

Central banks implemented QE programs, buying government securities and other assets to inject liquidity into the financial system, lower long-term interest rates, and support lending and investment.

Fiscal Policy Measures:

Stimulus Packages:

Governments launched large fiscal stimulus packages to boost demand and counteract the recessionary effects of the crisis. These included tax cuts, increased public spending, and financial support for distressed industries.

Bailouts and Support:

Financial institutions deemed critical to the financial system received direct bailouts and support, including capital injections and guarantees to stabilize the banking sector.

Regulatory Reforms:

Dodd-Frank Act:

In the U.S., the Dodd-Frank Wall Street Reform and Consumer Protection Act was enacted to improve regulatory oversight, enhance consumer protection, and reduce systemic risk.

Basel III:

The Basel Committee on Banking Supervision introduced Basel III, a set of international regulatory standards aimed at strengthening bank capital requirements, improving risk management, and enhancing liquidity buffers.

Immediate Impact on Inflation

Deflationary Pressures:

Demand Shock:

The crisis led to a sharp decline in consumer and business confidence, reducing spending and investment. This demand shock created deflationary pressures as excess capacity and falling demand pushed prices downward.

Credit Crunch:

The collapse of financial institutions and the resulting credit crunch restricted access to credit, further dampening economic activity and contributing to deflation.

Central Bank Interventions:

Preventing Deflation:

Central banks' aggressive monetary easing aimed to counteract deflationary pressures by stimulating demand and encouraging borrowing and spending. QE programs increased the money supply, aiming to boost inflation and economic activity.

Low Inflation:

Despite these efforts, inflation remained subdued in many advanced economies. The slack in labor markets, with high unemployment rates, kept wage growth low, limiting inflationary pressures.

Long-Term Impacts on Inflation

Persistent Low Inflation:

Advanced Economies:

In many advanced economies, inflation remained below target for an extended period following the crisis. Factors such as weak demand, slow wage growth, and the anchoring of inflation expectations contributed to this persistence.

Secular Stagnation:

The concept of secular stagnation, where economies experience prolonged periods of low growth and low inflation, gained traction as a possible explanation for the post-crisis economic environment.

Divergent Outcomes in Emerging Markets:

Varied Inflation Rates:

Emerging markets experienced divergent inflation outcomes. Some countries faced inflationary pressures due to currency depreciation, capital outflows, and rising commodity prices. Others managed to maintain relative price stability through effective monetary and fiscal policies.

Policy Responses:

The effectiveness of policy responses varied across emerging markets. Countries with stronger institutions, better fiscal positions, and credible central banks managed inflation better than those with structural weaknesses.

Structural Changes and Inflation Dynamics:

Deleveraging:

The post-crisis period saw significant deleveraging by households and businesses, reducing demand and contributing to low inflation. This process of reducing debt levels was slow and painful, limiting economic growth and price pressures.

Technological Advances:

Technological advancements, particularly in automation and digitalization, contributed to productivity gains and cost reductions, exerting downward pressure on prices.

Case Studies: Country Responses and Inflation Outcomes

United States:

Monetary Policy:

The Federal Reserve's QE programs and low interest rates supported economic recovery but did not lead to the feared inflation spike. Inflation remained below target for several years post-crisis.

Fiscal Policy:

The American Recovery and Reinvestment Act of 2009 provided significant fiscal stimulus, boosting demand and helping to stabilize the economy. However, fiscal austerity measures in subsequent years limited long-term inflationary pressures.

Eurozone:

ECB's Response:

The ECB's response included interest rate cuts, QE, and targeted long-term refinancing operations (TLTROs). Despite these measures, the Eurozone struggled with low inflation, partly due to structural issues and fiscal constraints.

Divergent Inflation:

Inflation rates varied across Eurozone member states. Countries like Germany maintained low inflation, while others, such as Greece and Spain, faced deflationary pressures due to severe economic contractions and austerity measures.

Japan:

Continued Deflationary Pressures:

The BOJ's aggressive monetary easing, including QQE and YCC, aimed to overcome entrenched deflation. While these measures provided some support, Japan continued to struggle with low inflation and weak economic growth.

Structural Challenges:

Japan's aging population, high public debt, and structural inefficiencies contributed to persistent deflationary pressures.

Lessons Learned and Future Directions

Importance of Timely and Coordinated Responses:

The GFC highlighted the need for timely and coordinated monetary and fiscal policy responses to manage deflationary pressures and support economic recovery. Delays or inadequate responses can exacerbate economic downturns and prolong low inflation.

Role of Central Banks:

Central banks play a critical role in managing inflation during crises. However, unconventional monetary policies, such as QE and negative interest rates, come with limitations and potential side effects, necessitating a careful balance between short-term benefits and long-term risks.

Fiscal Policy's Complementary Role:

Effective fiscal policy is essential in complementing monetary measures. Fiscal stimulus can boost demand and support economic recovery, while fiscal discipline ensures long-term sustainability and prevents inflationary spirals.

Structural Reforms:

Structural reforms aimed at improving productivity, enhancing labor market flexibility, and addressing supply-side constraints are crucial for maintaining price stability and supporting sustainable growth.

Global Coordination:

The interconnected nature of the global economy underscores the importance of international coordination in managing financial crises and their inflationary impacts. Collaborative efforts can help stabilize global markets and prevent contagion.

Conclusion

The 2008 Global Financial Crisis had profound and lasting effects on inflation worldwide. The crisis underscored the importance of coordinated policy responses, the critical role of central banks, and the need for structural reforms to ensure long-term economic stability. By examining the crisis and its aftermath, we gain valuable insights into the complexities of managing inflation in a globalized and interconnected economy.

In the following chapters, we will explore the relationship between inflation and income inequality, the impact of inflation on global trade, and the broader social and economic consequences of inflation, providing a comprehensive understanding of its multifaceted nature in the global economy.

Chapter 8
Inflation and Income Inequality

Introduction

Inflation and income inequality are two critical issues that significantly impact economic stability and social welfare. This chapter delves into the complex relationship between inflation and income inequality, examining how inflation disproportionately affects various socio-economic groups and exploring policies that can mitigate these effects. By understanding the nuances of this relationship, policymakers can develop strategies to promote inclusive economic growth and social equity.

Understanding Income Inequality

Definition and Measurement:

Income Inequality:

Income inequality refers to the uneven distribution of income across a population. It is typically measured using indices such as the Gini coefficient, which ranges from 0 (perfect equality) to 1 (maximum inequality), and income quintile or decile ratios.

Wealth Inequality:

Beyond income, wealth inequality considers the distribution of assets like property, stocks, and savings, which often reveals even greater disparities.

Factors Contributing to Income Inequality:

Economic Factors:

Economic growth patterns, technological advancements, and globalization can influence income distribution. For instance, technological changes may disproportionately benefit skilled workers, widening the income gap.

Social and Institutional Factors:

Education, access to healthcare, social mobility, and labor market institutions play significant roles in shaping income distribution.

Policy Factors:

Tax policies, social welfare programs, and labor market regulations can either mitigate or exacerbate income inequality.

How Inflation Affects Different Socio-Economic Groups

Erosion of Purchasing Power:

Fixed Income Groups:

Inflation erodes the purchasing power of fixed-income groups, such as retirees on pensions and workers with stagnant wages. These groups may struggle to maintain their standard of living as prices rise.

Low-Income Households:

Low-income households spend a larger proportion of their income on necessities like food, housing, and transportation. Inflation in these essential goods and services disproportionately impacts their budgets, increasing financial stress.

Asset Prices and Wealth Distribution:

Inflation and Asset Prices:

Inflation can lead to higher prices for real assets like property and stocks. Wealthier individuals who own these assets may see their wealth increase, further widening the income and wealth gap.

Savings Erosion:

Inflation diminishes the real value of savings, particularly affecting low- and middle-income households with fewer investment opportunities. This erosion of savings can exacerbate wealth inequality.

Debt Burden:

Fixed-Rate Debt:

Inflation can reduce the real burden of fixed-rate debt, benefiting borrowers who can repay their loans with less valuable money. However, low-income individuals may have limited access to credit markets.

Variable-Rate Debt:

Conversely, inflation can lead to higher interest rates on variable-rate debt, increasing repayment burdens for those with such loans, often affecting lower-income borrowers.

Wage-Price Spiral:

Wage Negotiations:

Inflation can lead to demands for higher wages as workers seek to maintain their purchasing power. However, not all workers have the bargaining power to secure wage increases, exacerbating income disparities.

Unemployment Risks:

Efforts to curb inflation through tight monetary policies can lead to higher unemployment, disproportionately affecting lower-skilled and lower-income workers.

Case Studies: Inflation and Inequality in Different Contexts

United States:

1970s Inflation:

The high inflation of the 1970s eroded purchasing power, particularly affecting low- and middle-income households. Wealthier individuals with assets that appreciated in value saw their relative wealth increase.

Recent Trends:

In the post-2008 period, inflation remained low, but asset prices surged due to monetary policies like quantitative easing. This asset inflation benefited wealthier households, contributing to increased wealth inequality.

Latin America:

Hyperinflation in Brazil:

During the 1980s and early 1990s, Brazil experienced hyperinflation, severely impacting low-income households. Government stabilization programs, including currency reform and fiscal discipline, eventually restored stability but required significant social and economic adjustments.

Argentina's Inflation:

Persistent inflation in Argentina has disproportionately affected low-income households. Efforts to control inflation through monetary and fiscal policies have had mixed success, highlighting the challenges of achieving price stability and social equity.

Africa:

Zimbabwe's Hyperinflation:

The hyperinflation in Zimbabwe during the late 2000s devastated the economy, with the poor bearing the brunt of the crisis. Essential goods became unaffordable, and savings were wiped out, exacerbating poverty and inequality.

Policies to Mitigate the Effects of Inflation on Income Inequality

Monetary Policy:

Inflation Targeting:

Central banks can adopt inflation targeting to maintain price stability, reducing uncertainty and protecting the purchasing power of low- and middle-income households.

Inclusive Monetary Policies:

Policies that support economic growth and job creation can help mitigate the adverse effects of inflation on unemployment and income inequality.

Fiscal Policy:

Progressive Taxation:

Implementing progressive tax systems can help redistribute income and reduce inequality. Higher taxes on wealth and capital gains can offset the benefits that inflation provides to asset owners.

Social Safety Nets:

Strengthening social safety nets, such as unemployment benefits, food assistance programs, and social security, can protect vulnerable groups from the adverse effects of inflation.

Public Investment:

Investing in education, healthcare, and infrastructure can promote economic opportunities and social mobility, helping to reduce structural inequalities.

Labor Market Policies:

Minimum Wage Policies:

Adjusting minimum wages to keep pace with inflation can protect low-income workers' purchasing power and reduce income disparities.

Collective Bargaining:

Supporting collective bargaining rights can empower workers to negotiate better wages and working conditions, mitigating the impact of inflation on their incomes.

Regulatory Measures:

Price Controls:

In extreme cases, temporary price controls on essential goods and services can protect low-income households from sudden price spikes. However, such measures must be carefully designed to avoid market distortions and shortages.

Consumer Protection:

Strengthening consumer protection laws can prevent exploitative practices that disproportionately harm low-income consumers during inflationary periods.

International Coordination:

Global Cooperation:

International cooperation on monetary and fiscal policies can help stabilize global markets and prevent the spillover effects of inflation and inequality.

Development Assistance:

Providing development assistance to low-income countries can support their efforts to achieve stable inflation and inclusive growth.

Conclusion

Inflation and income inequality are intricately linked, with inflation disproportionately affecting different socio-economic groups and exacerbating existing inequalities. By understanding this relationship, policymakers can design and implement effective strategies to mitigate the adverse effects of inflation on vulnerable populations. Through a combination of inclusive monetary and fiscal policies, progressive taxation, social safety nets, and labor market reforms, it is possible to promote economic stability and social equity.

In the subsequent chapters, we will continue to explore the broader impacts of inflation on global trade, economic growth, and social well-being, providing a comprehensive understanding of its multifaceted nature in the global economy.

Chapter 9
The Supply Chain and Inflation

Introduction

The global supply chain is a complex network that plays a vital role in the production and distribution of goods and services worldwide. Disruptions to this network can significantly impact inflation, influencing prices from raw materials to finished products. This chapter explores the intricate relationship between supply chain dynamics and inflation, focusing on how disruptions, such as the COVID-19 pandemic, have affected inflation and what measures can be taken to ensure supply chain stability and mitigate inflationary pressures.

Understanding the Global Supply Chain

Definition and Components:

Supply Chain:

The global supply chain encompasses all processes involved in producing and delivering goods and services, from raw material extraction to final delivery to consumers. It includes suppliers, manufacturers, logistics providers, and retailers.

Key Components:

The supply chain involves sourcing raw materials, manufacturing and production, warehousing, transportation, and distribution. Each stage adds value and incurs costs that contribute to the final price of goods.

Importance of Efficiency:

Cost Control:

Efficient supply chains minimize costs through optimized logistics, economies of scale, and just-in-time inventory management, helping to keep prices stable.

Global Integration:

The integration of global supply chains allows for the sourcing of materials and production in the most cost-effective locations, contributing to lower prices and enhanced economic efficiency.

Supply Chain Disruptions and Their Impact on Inflation

Types of Disruptions:

Natural Disasters:

Events such as earthquakes, floods, and hurricanes can damage infrastructure, disrupt production, and impede transportation, leading to supply shortages and price increases.

Geopolitical Events:

Trade wars, tariffs, and political instability can disrupt trade routes, increase costs, and lead to supply shortages, driving up prices.

Pandemics:

Health crises like the COVID-19 pandemic can cause widespread disruptions, affecting production, labor availability, and logistics, resulting in significant supply chain bottlenecks and inflationary pressures.

The COVID-19 Pandemic Case Study:

Initial Shock:

The pandemic caused widespread factory shutdowns, reduced labor availability, and disrupted transportation networks, leading to immediate supply shortages and increased costs.

Demand Shifts:

Changes in consumer behavior, such as increased demand for home goods and medical supplies, exacerbated supply chain pressures and led to price spikes in certain sectors.

Logistical Challenges:

Port closures, container shortages, and shipping delays created bottlenecks, further straining supply chains and contributing to inflation.

Raw Material Shortages:

Disruptions in the supply of key raw materials, such as semiconductors and lumber, affected production across multiple industries, driving up costs and prices.

Impact on Different Sectors:

Consumer Goods:

Shortages and increased costs for raw materials and transportation led to higher prices for consumer goods, including electronics, appliances, and furniture.

Automotive Industry:

The semiconductor shortage severely impacted car production, leading to reduced supply and higher prices for vehicles.

Food and Agriculture:

Disruptions in agricultural supply chains, including labor shortages and transportation challenges, contributed to higher food prices.

Measures to Ensure Supply Chain Stability

Diversification and Resilience:

Supplier Diversification:

Reducing reliance on single suppliers or regions by diversifying sourcing can mitigate risks and ensure a more stable supply of materials and components.

Resilient Infrastructure:

Investing in resilient infrastructure, including robust transportation networks and warehousing capacity, can help absorb shocks and maintain supply chain continuity.

Technological Advancements:

Digitalization:

Implementing digital technologies, such as blockchain, IoT, and AI, can enhance supply chain visibility, improve tracking, and enable more efficient management of inventory and logistics.

Automation:

Increasing automation in manufacturing and logistics can reduce dependence on labor and improve efficiency, helping to maintain stable production and distribution during disruptions.

Strategic Stockpiling:

Buffer Stocks:

Maintaining strategic reserves of critical raw materials and finished goods can provide a buffer against supply chain disruptions, reducing the risk of shortages and price spikes.

Inventory Management:

Adopting flexible inventory management practices, such as just-in-case inventory, can balance efficiency with the need for resilience.

Collaboration and Coordination:

Public-Private Partnerships:

Collaboration between governments and private sector entities can enhance supply chain resilience through coordinated efforts, shared resources, and strategic planning.

Global Cooperation:

International cooperation on trade policies, logistics standards, and crisis management can facilitate smoother global supply chain operations and mitigate the impact of disruptions.

Policy Measures:

Trade Policies:

Implementing trade policies that promote open markets and reduce barriers can enhance supply chain efficiency and stability. However, protectionist measures can exacerbate disruptions and inflation.

Regulation and Oversight:

Governments can implement regulations to ensure fair practices, prevent price gouging, and maintain competitive markets during supply chain disruptions.

Case Studies of Successful Supply Chain Management

Apple Inc.:

Supplier Diversification:

Apple has diversified its supplier base across multiple countries to reduce dependence on any single region. This strategy has helped mitigate risks associated with regional disruptions.

Technological Integration:

Apple employs advanced technology for supply chain management, including sophisticated forecasting and inventory systems, ensuring efficient production and distribution.

Toyota:

Just-In-Time (JIT):

Toyota's JIT inventory system minimizes waste and reduces inventory costs by aligning production closely with demand. This approach has historically enhanced efficiency but requires robust risk management to handle disruptions.

Resilience Strategies:

After the 2011 Fukushima earthquake, Toyota enhanced its supply chain resilience by increasing buffer stocks and collaborating closely with suppliers to ensure continuity.

Conclusion

The global supply chain is a critical factor in the inflation equation, with disruptions having significant impacts on prices and economic stability. Events like the COVID-19 pandemic have highlighted the vulnerabilities in supply chains and the resulting inflationary pressures. To mitigate these effects and ensure stability, a combination of diversification, technological advancements, strategic stockpiling, and coordinated policy measures is essential.

Understanding the interplay between supply chain dynamics and inflation is crucial for policymakers, businesses, and consumers. By enhancing supply chain resilience and efficiency, it is possible to reduce the risk of inflationary spikes and support sustainable economic growth.

In the following chapters, we will continue to explore the broader impacts of inflation on global trade, economic growth, and social well-being, providing a comprehensive understanding of its multifaceted nature in the global economy.

Chapter 10
Technology's Impact on Inflation

Introduction

Technology has revolutionized various sectors of the economy, profoundly influencing inflation. From the rise of e-commerce to advancements in manufacturing, digital transformation and innovation are reshaping the inflation landscape. This chapter delves into the myriad ways technology impacts inflation, examining both the deflationary and inflationary forces at play. By understanding these dynamics, we can better anticipate future inflation trends and develop effective economic policies.

The Deflationary Impact of Technology

Productivity Gains:

Automation and Efficiency:

Technological advancements in automation, robotics, and artificial intelligence (AI) have significantly increased productivity in manufacturing and services. Higher productivity reduces production costs, which can lead to lower prices for consumers.

Digitalization:

The digitalization of processes, from supply chain management to customer service, enhances efficiency, reduces waste, and cuts operational costs. These savings can be passed on to consumers in the form of lower prices.

E-Commerce and Price Transparency:

Competitive Pricing:

The rise of e-commerce platforms like Amazon and Alibaba has intensified price competition. Consumers can easily compare prices online, forcing retailers to offer competitive pricing, which helps keep inflation in check.

Lower Operating Costs:

E-commerce reduces the need for physical retail spaces and lowers associated costs such as rent, utilities, and staffing. These cost savings can contribute to lower prices for online consumers.

Innovation and Product Improvement:

Technological Innovation:

Continuous technological innovation leads to the development of new and improved products at lower costs. The rapid pace of innovation can result in frequent product updates and lower prices for older models.

Moore's Law:

The principle that the number of transistors on a microchip doubles approximately every two years, while the cost of computing power halves, illustrates how technological advancements can drive down prices in the electronics sector.

Supply Chain Optimization:

Just-In-Time (JIT) Inventory:

Technologies such as IoT and AI enable more accurate demand forecasting and inventory management, reducing the need for excess stock and minimizing storage costs.

Blockchain:

Blockchain technology enhances transparency and traceability in supply chains, reducing fraud, improving efficiency, and lowering transaction costs, which can contribute to lower prices.

The Inflationary Impact of Technology

Initial Investment Costs:

Capital Expenditure:

The adoption of new technologies often requires significant initial investment in equipment, software, and training. These costs can be passed on to consumers in the form of higher prices, at least initially.

Research and Development (R&D):

High R&D expenditures necessary for technological innovation can lead to higher prices for cutting-edge products as companies seek to recoup their investments.

Skilled Labor Shortages:

Demand for Skilled Workers:

Advanced technologies often require specialized skills, leading to increased demand for skilled labor. This can drive up wages for tech-savvy workers, potentially contributing to higher production costs and inflation.

Education and Training Costs:

Investments in education and training to develop the necessary skills for a technologically advanced workforce can also contribute to higher costs in the economy.

Network Effects and Market Power:

Monopolistic Tendencies:

Technology companies can achieve significant market power through network effects, where the value of a product or service increases with the number of users. Dominant players may exert pricing power, leading to higher prices.

Barriers to Entry:

High barriers to entry in technology-intensive industries can limit competition and allow incumbent firms to maintain higher prices.

Balancing Deflationary and Inflationary Forces

Case Studies:

Consumer Electronics:

Smartphones:

The smartphone industry exemplifies the balance between deflationary and inflationary forces. While the cost of individual components has decreased due to technological advancements, initial R&D investments and the demand for cutting-edge features keep prices high.

TVs and Laptops:

Prices for TVs and laptops have steadily decreased over time due to improvements in manufacturing efficiency and competition. However, new models with advanced features are often introduced at higher price points.

Automotive Industry:

Electric Vehicles (EVs):

The EV market is influenced by both deflationary and inflationary forces. Technological advancements in battery production and economies of scale are reducing costs, but initial investments and high R&D expenditures keep prices relatively high.

Automation and AI:

The adoption of automation and AI in car manufacturing increases productivity and reduces costs, contributing to lower prices. However, the need for skilled labor and technological infrastructure can counterbalance these deflationary effects.

Healthcare:

Medical Technology:

Innovations in medical technology, such as telemedicine, AI diagnostics, and robotic surgery, improve efficiency and outcomes. While these advancements can reduce long-term healthcare costs, initial investments and the demand for highly skilled practitioners can drive up prices.

Pharmaceuticals:

The pharmaceutical industry benefits from technological advancements in drug development and production, potentially lowering costs. However, high R&D costs and regulatory requirements can lead to higher prices for new medications.

Policy Implications and Strategies

Encouraging Innovation:

R&D Incentives:

Governments can provide tax incentives, grants, and subsidies to encourage R&D and innovation, helping to offset initial costs and promote technological advancements that contribute to long-term deflationary effects.

Public-Private Partnerships:

Collaborations between public institutions and private companies can drive innovation and efficiency, particularly in sectors like healthcare and infrastructure.

Education and Workforce Development:

Skill Development:

Investing in education and training programs to develop a skilled workforce can help meet the demand for specialized labor in technology-intensive industries, mitigating inflationary pressures from wage increases.

Lifelong Learning:

Promoting lifelong learning and continuous skill development can ensure that workers remain adaptable to technological changes, reducing the risk of labor market mismatches.

Regulation and Competition:

Antitrust Measures:

Implementing and enforcing antitrust regulations can prevent monopolistic practices and promote competition, helping to keep prices in check in technology-driven markets.

Regulatory Frameworks:

Developing regulatory frameworks that support innovation while protecting consumers can balance the benefits of technological advancements with the need for fair pricing.

Supporting SMEs and Startups:

Access to Capital:

Providing access to financing and venture capital for small and medium-sized enterprises (SMEs) and startups can foster innovation and competition, contributing to deflationary effects through increased market dynamism.

Innovation Hubs:

Establishing innovation hubs and incubators can support the growth of new technology companies, promoting a diverse and competitive market landscape.

Conclusion

Technology plays a crucial role in shaping inflation, exerting both deflationary and inflationary pressures on the economy. While advancements in automation, digitalization, and e-commerce drive down costs and prices, initial investments, skilled labor shortages, and market power can contribute to higher prices. Understanding the complex interplay between these forces is essential for policymakers, businesses, and consumers.

By fostering innovation, investing in education and workforce development, promoting competition, and supporting SMEs, it is possible to harness the deflationary benefits of technology while mitigating its inflationary impacts. In the following chapters, we will continue to explore the broader impacts of inflation on global trade, economic growth, and social well-being, providing a comprehensive understanding of its multifaceted nature in the global economy.

Chapter 11
Currency Wars and Competitive Devaluation

Introduction

In a globally interconnected economy, currency wars—where countries competitively devalue their currencies to gain trade advantages—can have significant inflationary consequences. This chapter examines instances of competitive devaluation, exploring their motivations, mechanisms, and impacts on global inflation dynamics. By understanding the complex interplay between currency policies and inflation, we can better appreciate the broader implications for economic stability and international relations.

Understanding Currency Wars and Competitive Devaluation

Definition and Motivations:

Currency War:

A currency war occurs when countries deliberately devalue their currencies to boost exports by making their goods cheaper on the international market. This can lead to a cycle of competitive devaluations as countries retaliate against each other.

Competitive Devaluation:

Competitive devaluation involves countries actively reducing the value of their currency through monetary policy, foreign exchange intervention, or other measures to gain a trade advantage.

Mechanisms of Devaluation:

Monetary Policy:

Central banks can lower interest rates to reduce the currency's value, making it less attractive to foreign investors and thus cheaper in foreign exchange markets.

Foreign Exchange Intervention:

Governments or central banks can directly intervene in the foreign exchange market by selling their own currency and buying foreign currencies, increasing the supply and decreasing the value of their currency.

Quantitative Easing (QE):

QE involves large-scale purchases of government bonds or other financial assets by the central bank, increasing the money supply and putting downward pressure on the currency's value.

Historical Instances of Currency Wars

The Great Depression (1930s):

Beggar-Thy-Neighbor Policies:

During the Great Depression, several countries, including the United States and the United Kingdom, devalued their currencies to boost exports and combat unemployment. These policies, aimed at gaining competitive trade advantages, led to retaliatory devaluations and trade barriers, exacerbating global economic instability.

Gold Standard Collapse:

The competitive devaluations and trade restrictions contributed to the collapse of the gold standard, further destabilizing international financial systems.

Post-Financial Crisis (2008-2010s):

Global Financial Crisis:

In the aftermath of the 2008 financial crisis, countries like the United States, Japan, and the Eurozone implemented aggressive monetary policies, including QE, to stimulate their economies. These actions led to accusations of currency manipulation and fears of a new currency war.

"Currency War" Term:

The term "currency war" gained prominence after Brazilian Finance Minister Guido Mantega accused developed countries of engaging in competitive devaluations to boost exports at the expense of emerging economies.

Impact of Competitive Devaluation on Global Inflation Dynamics

Imported Inflation:

Weaker Currency:

A weaker currency makes imports more expensive, leading to higher prices for imported goods and services. This can contribute to overall inflation, especially in countries heavily reliant on imports for essential goods like food, energy, and raw materials.

Pass-Through Effect:

The extent of imported inflation depends on the pass-through effect, which is the degree to which exchange rate changes translate into domestic price changes. Factors influencing the pass-through effect include the structure of the economy, pricing power of firms, and monetary policy responses.

Export-Led Growth and Inflation:

Export Competitiveness:

Competitive devaluation can boost export competitiveness by making domestic goods cheaper on the global market, leading to increased demand for exports. This can stimulate economic growth but may also contribute to inflation if demand outstrips supply.

Demand-Pull Inflation:

Increased export demand can lead to higher production and employment, boosting domestic income and consumption.

This can result in demand-pull inflation, where higher demand drives up prices.

Monetary Policy Responses:

Interest Rate Adjustments:

Central banks may adjust interest rates to counteract inflationary pressures from devaluation. Higher interest rates can attract foreign capital, supporting the currency but potentially dampening economic growth.

Inflation Targeting:

Countries with explicit inflation targets may face challenges in balancing exchange rate stability and inflation control, particularly during periods of competitive devaluation.

Global Spillover Effects:

Trade Partners:

Competitive devaluations can have spillover effects on trade partners, affecting their export competitiveness and inflation dynamics. For example, if a major trading partner devalues its currency, other countries may experience reduced export demand and increased import prices, influencing their inflation rates.

Financial Markets:

Currency wars can lead to increased volatility in financial markets, affecting investor confidence and capital flows. This can impact inflation through changes in asset prices, investment, and consumption patterns.

Case Studies: Competitive Devaluation and Inflation

Japan's Abenomics:

Economic Context:

In the early 2010s, Japan faced deflation and stagnation. Prime Minister Shinzo Abe implemented a policy mix known as "Abenomics," which included aggressive monetary easing to devalue the yen and boost exports.

Inflation Impact:

The yen's devaluation contributed to higher import prices, particularly for energy, leading to moderate inflation. However, structural issues and weak domestic demand limited the overall inflationary impact.

China's Yuan Devaluation (2015):

Economic Context:

In 2015, China's economy faced slowing growth and financial market turbulence. The People's Bank of China devalued the yuan to support export competitiveness and stabilize economic growth.

Inflation Impact:

The devaluation increased import prices, contributing to inflationary pressures. However, China's extensive foreign exchange reserves and capital controls helped manage the impact on overall price stability.

Policy Measures to Mitigate Inflationary Consequences

Coordination and Cooperation:

International Agreements:

International cooperation through forums like the G20 can help mitigate the risks of currency wars by promoting coordinated policy responses and discouraging competitive devaluations.

IMF Role:

The International Monetary Fund (IMF) can play a crucial role in monitoring exchange rate policies, providing policy advice, and offering financial assistance to countries facing balance of payments crises.

Domestic Policy Adjustments:

Monetary Policy:

Central banks can use interest rate adjustments, inflation targeting, and other monetary tools to manage inflationary pressures arising from currency devaluations.

Fiscal Policy:

Governments can implement fiscal measures, such as targeted subsidies or tax adjustments, to mitigate the impact of higher import prices on vulnerable populations.

Structural Reforms:

Economic Diversification:

Diversifying the economy and reducing reliance on imports can help mitigate the impact of imported inflation.

Investing in domestic industries and developing alternative supply chains can enhance resilience.

Competitiveness Improvements:

Enhancing productivity and competitiveness through innovation, infrastructure investment, and workforce development can reduce the need for competitive devaluations and support stable economic growth.

Conclusion

Currency wars and competitive devaluation have significant implications for global inflation dynamics. While devaluing currencies can provide short-term trade advantages, they can also lead to imported inflation, demand-pull inflation, and broader economic instability. Understanding these complex interactions is crucial for policymakers, businesses, and consumers.

By promoting international cooperation, adjusting domestic policies, and implementing structural reforms, countries can mitigate the inflationary consequences of currency wars and support stable, sustainable economic growth. In the following chapters, we will continue to explore the broader impacts of inflation on global trade, economic growth, and social well-being, providing a comprehensive understanding of its multifaceted nature in the global economy.

Chapter 12
The Energy Sector and Inflation

Introduction

Energy prices play a critical role in shaping inflation dynamics worldwide. Fluctuations in the cost of oil, gas, and renewable energy sources can have profound impacts on the broader economy, influencing the prices of goods and services across various sectors. This chapter examines the relationship between the energy sector and inflation, exploring how changes in energy prices drive inflation and what the future holds for energy-related inflation in a transitioning energy landscape.

The Role of Energy Prices in Inflation

Direct and Indirect Effects:

Direct Effects:

Energy prices directly affect the cost of transportation, heating, electricity, and industrial processes. When energy prices rise, these costs increase, leading to higher prices for consumers and businesses.

Indirect Effects:

Energy prices indirectly influence the cost of goods and services by affecting production and transportation costs. Higher energy costs can lead to increased prices for raw materials, manufacturing, and distribution, contributing to overall inflation.

Inflationary Mechanisms:

Cost-Push Inflation:

Rising energy prices can lead to cost-push inflation, where increased production costs are passed on to consumers in the form of higher prices. This type of inflation occurs when the supply of goods and services is constrained by higher input costs.

Second-Round Effects:

Initial increases in energy prices can trigger second-round effects, where higher costs for goods and services lead to higher wages and other costs, creating a cycle of rising prices and wages.

Historical Context: Energy Prices and Inflation

Oil Price Shocks:

1970s Oil Crises:

The oil price shocks of the 1970s, caused by geopolitical events such as the Arab oil embargo and the Iranian Revolution, led to significant increases in oil prices. These shocks resulted in widespread cost-push inflation, contributing to stagflation—a period of high inflation and stagnant economic growth.

1990s Oil Price Fluctuations:

In the 1990s, oil prices experienced significant fluctuations due to events such as the Gulf War and changes in OPEC production policies. These fluctuations had varying impacts on inflation, with periods of high oil prices contributing to higher inflation rates.

Recent Trends:

2000s Commodity Boom:

In the early 2000s, rising demand from emerging economies, particularly China, led to a commodity boom and higher energy prices. This contributed to increased inflationary pressures globally.

2020s Energy Transition:

The current decade is marked by a transition to renewable energy sources, changing demand dynamics, and geopolitical tensions. These factors continue to influence energy prices and their impact on inflation.

Fluctuations in Oil Prices and Inflation

Oil Market Dynamics:

Supply and Demand:

Oil prices are influenced by global supply and demand dynamics. Factors such as economic growth, technological advancements, and geopolitical events can impact both supply and demand, leading to price fluctuations.

OPEC and Non-OPEC Producers:

The Organization of the Petroleum Exporting Countries (OPEC) plays a significant role in oil price determination through production quotas and policies. Non-OPEC producers, such as the United States (with its shale oil production), also influence the market.

Inflationary Impact of Oil Price Changes:

Transportation Costs:

Higher oil prices increase transportation costs, affecting the prices of goods that rely on shipping, trucking, and aviation. This can lead to higher prices for consumer goods and services.

Production Costs:

Industries that rely heavily on oil, such as chemicals, plastics, and manufacturing, face higher production costs when oil prices rise. These costs are often passed on to consumers, contributing to inflation.

Energy Bills:

Households and businesses experience higher energy bills when oil prices increase, reducing disposable income and potentially leading to higher prices for other goods and services as businesses pass on costs.

Case Study: The 2008 Oil Price Spike:

Economic Context:

In 2008, oil prices surged to record highs, driven by strong global demand and supply constraints. Prices peaked at over $140 per barrel, contributing to increased inflationary pressures.

Inflation Impact:

The spike in oil prices led to higher transportation and production costs, contributing to rising inflation rates in many countries. The subsequent financial crisis and economic downturn moderated these pressures, highlighting the complex interplay between energy prices and inflation.

The Influence of Natural Gas Prices on Inflation

Market Dynamics:

Global Supply and Demand:

Natural gas prices are influenced by factors such as global supply and demand, weather patterns, and geopolitical events. The development of liquefied natural gas (LNG) has increased global trade and market integration.

Regional Differences:

Unlike oil, natural gas prices can vary significantly across regions due to transportation constraints and differing market structures. This can lead to varied inflationary impacts depending on regional supply and demand conditions.

Inflationary Impact of Natural Gas Price Changes:

Heating and Electricity Costs:

Natural gas is a key source of heating and electricity generation. Higher natural gas prices can lead to increased energy bills for households and businesses, contributing to inflation.

Industrial Costs:

Industries such as chemicals, fertilizers, and manufacturing rely on natural gas as a feedstock and energy source. Rising natural gas prices can increase production costs and lead to higher prices for finished goods.

Case Study: European Energy Crisis (2021-2022):

Supply Constraints:

In 2021 and 2022, Europe faced a significant energy crisis due to supply constraints, geopolitical tensions, and rising demand. Natural gas prices surged, leading to higher energy costs.

Inflation Impact:

The spike in natural gas prices contributed to higher inflation rates across Europe, with increased energy bills affecting both households and businesses. Governments implemented measures such as subsidies and price caps to mitigate the impact on consumers.

The Role of Renewable Energy in Shaping Inflation

Transition to Renewables:

Growing Adoption:

The transition to renewable energy sources, such as solar, wind, and hydroelectric power, is accelerating globally. This shift is driven by environmental concerns, technological advancements, and policy incentives.

Cost Dynamics:

The costs of renewable energy technologies have been declining, with solar and wind power becoming increasingly competitive with fossil fuels. However, the initial investment and infrastructure development can be significant.

Inflationary and Deflationary Impacts:

Deflationary Potential:

As renewable energy becomes more cost-effective, it can lead to lower energy prices over the long term, contributing to deflationary pressures. Reduced dependence on volatile fossil fuel markets can enhance price stability.

Investment Costs:

The transition to renewable energy requires significant upfront investment in infrastructure, technology, and grid integration. These costs can be inflationary in the short term, particularly if they are passed on to consumers.

Case Study: Solar Energy Expansion:

Cost Reductions:

The cost of solar energy has declined dramatically over the past decade due to technological advancements, economies of scale, and government incentives. This has made solar power increasingly competitive with traditional energy sources.

Inflation Impact:

In regions with significant solar energy adoption, the reduced cost of electricity can help mitigate inflationary pressures. However, the initial investments in solar infrastructure can contribute to higher prices in the short term.

Future Outlook for Energy-Related Inflation

Energy Transition and Policy:

Climate Policies:

Governments worldwide are implementing policies to reduce carbon emissions and transition to renewable energy. These policies can influence energy prices and their impact on inflation, depending on their design and implementation.

Technological Innovation:

Continued innovation in energy technologies, including advancements in energy storage, grid management, and efficiency, can help stabilize energy prices and reduce inflationary pressures.

Geopolitical Factors:

Supply Chain Security:

Geopolitical events, such as conflicts, trade tensions, and sanctions, can disrupt energy supply chains and lead to price volatility. Ensuring secure and diversified energy supplies is crucial for managing inflation risks.

Energy Independence:

Efforts to achieve greater energy independence through domestic production and renewable energy can enhance resilience to global energy price fluctuations and reduce inflationary pressures.

Market Dynamics:

Demand Shifts:

Changes in global energy demand, driven by economic growth, technological adoption, and consumer behavior, will influence future energy prices and their impact on inflation.

Price Volatility:

Energy markets are inherently volatile due to factors such as weather patterns, geopolitical events, and technological disruptions. Managing this volatility is crucial for maintaining price stability and controlling inflation.

Conclusion

Energy prices are a major driver of inflation, with fluctuations in oil, gas, and renewable energy sources significantly impacting the broader economy. Understanding the relationship between the energy sector and inflation is crucial for policymakers, businesses, and consumers.

As the world transitions to renewable energy, the future of energy-related inflation will be shaped by technological advancements, policy decisions, and geopolitical factors. By promoting energy efficiency, investing in resilient infrastructure, and fostering innovation, it is possible to mitigate the inflationary impacts of energy price fluctuations and support sustainable economic growth.

In the following chapters, we will continue to explore the broader impacts of inflation on global trade, economic growth, and social well-being, providing a comprehensive understanding of its multifaceted nature in the global economy.

Chapter 13
Government Debt and Inflation

Introduction

High levels of government debt are often scrutinized for their potential to cause inflationary pressures. Understanding the relationship between fiscal policy, debt management, and inflation is critical for policymakers aiming to maintain economic stability. This chapter delves into how government debt can influence inflation, explores the mechanisms involved, and presents case studies from various countries to illustrate the complexities of this relationship.

The Relationship Between Government Debt and Inflation

Theoretical Foundations:

Demand-Pull Inflation:

High levels of government spending, particularly when financed by debt, can increase aggregate demand, leading to demand-pull inflation. When the economy is at or near full capacity, additional demand can push prices up.

Cost-Push Inflation:

Large debt can lead to higher interest rates as investors demand greater compensation for perceived risks. Higher interest rates increase borrowing costs for businesses and consumers, potentially leading to cost-push inflation.

Monetization of Debt:

If a government finances its debt by printing money (monetization), this increases the money supply and can lead to inflation. Central banks must manage this risk carefully to avoid hyperinflation scenarios.

Debt and Fiscal Policy:

Fiscal Deficits:

Persistent fiscal deficits, where government spending exceeds revenue, necessitate borrowing. Over time, high levels of borrowing can increase the debt-to-GDP ratio, influencing inflation expectations and economic stability.

Debt Sustainability:

The ability of a government to service its debt without resorting to excessive money printing or austerity measures is crucial for maintaining low inflation. Sustainable debt levels depend on economic growth, interest rates, and fiscal policies.

Historical Context: Government Debt and Inflation

Post-World War II Period:

War Debts:

After World War II, many countries faced high levels of debt. The response varied, with some nations experiencing inflationary pressures as they tried to reduce debt through economic growth and inflation.

Marshall Plan:

The United States' Marshall Plan helped Western European countries rebuild and stabilize their economies, which contributed to moderate inflation rates despite high initial debt levels.

1980s Debt Crisis:

Latin American Debt Crisis:

In the 1980s, many Latin American countries experienced severe debt crises, leading to hyperinflation in countries like Argentina and Brazil. The inability to service foreign debts led to currency devaluations and runaway inflation.

Austerity Measures:

Countries that implemented strict austerity measures and structural reforms, often under the guidance of the IMF, managed to stabilize their economies and reduce inflation over time.

Mechanisms Linking Government Debt and Inflation

Monetary Policy and Central Bank Independence:

Central Bank Credibility:

Independent central banks that focus on controlling inflation can help mitigate the inflationary impact of high government debt. Credibility in maintaining low inflation expectations is crucial.

Policy Coordination:

Effective coordination between fiscal and monetary policy is essential. When fiscal policy is expansionary, central banks may need to adopt tighter monetary policies to prevent inflation.

Inflation Expectations:

Role of Expectations:

If businesses and consumers expect future inflation due to high government debt, they may adjust their behavior accordingly. This can lead to a self-fulfilling prophecy where inflation expectations drive actual inflation.

Anchoring Expectations:

Central banks use tools like inflation targeting to anchor expectations. Clear communication and commitment to low inflation help prevent the de-anchoring of expectations even in the face of high debt.

Debt Composition and Structure:

Domestic vs. External Debt:

The composition of debt matters. External debt, especially in foreign currencies, can be more inflationary if it leads to currency depreciation and higher import prices. Domestic debt can be managed through monetary policy but still poses inflation risks.

Maturity Structure:

Short-term debt requires frequent refinancing, which can lead to higher interest rates and inflationary pressures if investors demand a risk premium. Long-term debt can mitigate refinancing risks but may carry higher interest costs.

Case Studies: Government Debt and Inflation

Japan:

Economic Context:

Japan has one of the highest debt-to-GDP ratios in the world, exceeding 250%. Despite this, Japan has experienced low inflation and even deflation for much of the past two decades.

Policy Response:

The Bank of Japan's aggressive monetary easing, combined with fiscal stimulus and structural reforms, has kept inflation low. Japan's unique situation highlights the importance of context and the interplay of various economic factors.

Greece:

Debt Crisis:

Greece's debt crisis in the early 2010s led to severe economic contraction and high inflation. The crisis was driven by high debt levels, fiscal mismanagement, and lack of competitiveness within the Eurozone.

Austerity and Reforms:

Austerity measures imposed by the EU and IMF aimed to reduce debt and stabilize the economy. While these measures helped reduce inflation, they also led to significant social and economic challenges.

Zimbabwe:

Hyperinflation:

Zimbabwe experienced one of the worst cases of hyperinflation in history in the late 2000s, with inflation rates reaching billions of percent. This was due to excessive money printing to finance government spending and a collapse in economic output.

Currency Reforms:

The introduction of a multi-currency system and later the reintroduction of the Zimbabwean dollar, alongside strict monetary policies, helped stabilize inflation but required significant economic restructuring.

Managing Government Debt to Control Inflation

Fiscal Discipline and Structural Reforms:

Balanced Budgets:

Maintaining balanced budgets and reducing fiscal deficits can help manage debt levels and prevent inflation. This often involves tough policy choices, including spending cuts and tax increases.

Economic Growth:

Promoting sustainable economic growth through structural reforms, investment in infrastructure, and human capital development can help manage debt levels and reduce inflationary pressures.

Monetary Policy Strategies:

Inflation Targeting:

Central banks can use inflation targeting to anchor expectations and control inflation. This involves setting clear inflation targets and using interest rates and other tools to achieve these targets.

Quantitative Easing:

In times of crisis, central banks may use quantitative easing (QE) to support the economy. While QE can help manage debt by lowering borrowing costs, it must be carefully managed to avoid long-term inflationary impacts.

Debt Management Techniques:

Debt Restructuring:

In cases of unsustainable debt, restructuring may be necessary. This can involve extending maturities, reducing interest rates, or writing off portions of the debt.

Diversified Financing:

Using a mix of financing sources, including domestic and international markets, can help manage risks and reduce the inflationary impact of debt.

Conclusion

The relationship between government debt and inflation is complex and influenced by various factors, including fiscal and monetary policies, economic context, and market dynamics. High levels of government debt can lead to inflationary pressures, but the outcomes depend on how debt is managed and the broader economic environment.

Case studies from around the world demonstrate different approaches to managing debt and controlling inflation. Successful strategies often involve a combination of fiscal discipline, monetary policy coordination, and structural reforms.

As we move forward, understanding the interplay between government debt and inflation will be crucial for maintaining economic stability and promoting sustainable growth. In the subsequent chapters, we will continue to explore the broader impacts of inflation on global trade, economic growth, and social well-being, providing a comprehensive understanding of its multifaceted nature in the global economy.

Chapter 14
Inflation Targeting
Successes and Failures

Introduction

Inflation targeting has become a widely adopted monetary policy framework used by central banks around the world. It involves setting an explicit target for the inflation rate and using interest rate adjustments and other monetary tools to achieve that target. This chapter explores the origins and principles of inflation targeting, evaluates its effectiveness through various case studies, and discusses the factors that contribute to its successes and failures.

The Concept of Inflation Targeting

Definition and Principles:

Inflation Targeting Framework:

Central banks set a specific inflation rate as the primary goal of monetary policy. The target is typically communicated clearly to the public, enhancing transparency and accountability.

Policy Tools:

To achieve the target, central banks primarily use interest rate adjustments, alongside other tools such as open market operations and reserve requirements. By raising or lowering interest rates, they influence economic activity and inflation.

Historical Background:

Early Adopters:

New Zealand was the first country to adopt inflation targeting in 1990, followed by Canada, the United Kingdom, and Sweden. These countries aimed to control inflation more effectively than previous policy frameworks had allowed.

Global Spread:

Over the decades, inflation targeting has been adopted by many advanced and emerging market economies, becoming a standard approach in modern central banking.

The Effectiveness of Inflation Targeting

Benefits and Successes:

Lower and More Stable Inflation:

Countries that adopted inflation targeting have generally experienced lower and more stable inflation rates compared to previous periods. The clear focus on inflation control helps anchor expectations and reduce volatility.

Enhanced Transparency and Accountability:

By setting explicit targets, central banks improve their communication with the public and financial markets. This transparency enhances the credibility of monetary policy and helps anchor inflation expectations.

Flexibility:

Inflation targeting allows central banks to respond flexibly to economic shocks. While the primary goal is price stability, many central banks also consider other factors such as employment and economic growth when making policy decisions.

Case Studies of Success:

New Zealand:

As the pioneer of inflation targeting, New Zealand successfully reduced its inflation rate from double digits in the 1980s to within the target range by the mid-1990s. The Reserve Bank of New Zealand's commitment to transparency and accountability played a key role in this success.

Canada:

The Bank of Canada adopted inflation targeting in 1991, setting a target range of 1-3%. The policy helped reduce inflation from over 5% in the early 1990s to stable levels within the target range, contributing to sustained economic growth and stability.

United Kingdom:

The Bank of England adopted inflation targeting in 1992. The framework successfully brought inflation under control, reducing it from high levels in the early 1990s to around the 2% target. This stability has supported economic growth and employment.

Shortcomings and Failures of Inflation Targeting

Challenges and Limitations:

Rigid Focus on Inflation:

In some cases, a strict focus on inflation targets can lead to suboptimal economic outcomes. For instance, excessively tight monetary policy to combat inflation can stifle economic growth and increase unemployment.

Financial Stability Concerns:

Inflation targeting does not directly address financial stability. Central banks focusing solely on inflation may overlook emerging financial imbalances and asset bubbles, which can lead to economic crises.

Global and Supply-Side Shocks:

Inflation targeting can be less effective in responding to global economic shocks or supply-side shocks, such as commodity price spikes or natural disasters, which can drive inflation beyond the control of domestic monetary policy.

Case Studies of Failure:

Argentina:

Argentina adopted inflation targeting in 2016, aiming to bring down high inflation rates. However, the policy failed to achieve its goals due to weak fiscal discipline, lack of central bank independence, and severe economic crises. Inflation remained persistently high, eroding confidence in the central bank.

Iceland:

Iceland's experience with inflation targeting in the early 2000s highlights the challenges of managing financial stability. While the Central Bank of Iceland focused on controlling inflation, it failed to address a rapidly growing financial sector and credit boom, leading to a severe financial crisis in 2008.

Turkey:

The Central Bank of Turkey adopted inflation targeting in 2006, but has struggled to maintain low and stable inflation. Political pressures, lack of central bank independence, and external economic shocks have undermined the effectiveness of the policy.

Best Practices and Lessons Learned

Key Success Factors:

Central Bank Independence:

Effective inflation targeting requires a high degree of central bank independence. Political interference can undermine the credibility and effectiveness of monetary policy.

Transparent Communication:

Clear and consistent communication of the inflation target and the central bank's actions helps anchor expectations and build public trust. Transparency reduces uncertainty and enhances policy effectiveness.

Flexible Framework:

While inflation targeting focuses on price stability, a flexible approach that also considers economic growth and employment can lead to better overall outcomes. Central banks should be prepared to adapt their policies in response to changing economic conditions.

Recommendations for Improvement:

Integrating Financial Stability:

Central banks should incorporate financial stability considerations into their inflation targeting frameworks. Monitoring and addressing financial imbalances can prevent crises that disrupt economic stability and inflation control.

Enhancing Coordination:

Coordination between fiscal and monetary policy is crucial for achieving macroeconomic stability. Fiscal discipline and supportive fiscal policies can complement inflation targeting efforts.

Adapting to New Challenges:

Central banks should continuously adapt their strategies to address emerging challenges, such as digital currencies, technological disruptions, and climate change. An evolving approach ensures that inflation targeting remains effective in a changing economic landscape.

Conclusion

Inflation targeting has proven to be a successful monetary policy framework for many countries, contributing to lower and more stable inflation, enhanced transparency, and improved economic outcomes. However, it is not without its challenges and limitations. The effectiveness of inflation targeting depends on central bank independence, transparent communication, flexibility, and the integration of financial stability considerations.

By learning from both successes and failures, central banks can refine their inflation targeting strategies to better address the complexities of modern economies. As we continue to explore the broader impacts of inflation on global trade, economic growth, and social well-being in subsequent chapters, understanding the nuances of inflation targeting will provide valuable insights into maintaining economic stability in a dynamic world.

Chapter 15
Social and Political Consequences of Inflation

Introduction

Inflation is not just an economic phenomenon; it has profound social and political ramifications. High inflation can erode purchasing power, exacerbate income inequality, and lead to widespread dissatisfaction among the populace. This chapter explores how inflation has influenced political stability and social structures through historical and contemporary examples. We examine the ways in which governments and societies respond to inflationary pressures and the resulting social and political consequences.

The Social Impact of Inflation

Erosion of Purchasing Power:

Cost of Living:

As prices rise, the cost of living increases, reducing the real income of households. This effect is particularly severe for those on fixed incomes, such as pensioners and low-wage workers.

Standard of Living:

Sustained inflation can diminish the standard of living by making essential goods and services unaffordable for many. This can lead to increased poverty and social inequality.

Income Inequality:

Wealth Distribution:

Inflation can disproportionately affect different socio-economic groups. Wealthier individuals often have assets that appreciate with inflation, such as real estate and stocks, while poorer individuals rely more on cash savings and fixed incomes, which lose value.

Wage-Price Spiral:

In high inflation environments, workers demand higher wages to keep up with rising prices, leading to a wage-price spiral. However, not all workers have the bargaining power to secure higher wages, increasing income inequality.

Social Unrest:

Public Protests:

When inflation erodes living standards, it can lead to widespread public protests and social unrest. People may take to the streets to demand higher wages, price controls, or government intervention.

Crime and Violence:

High inflation can contribute to higher crime rates and violence as people struggle to maintain their livelihoods.

Economic desperation can lead to increased theft, robbery, and other criminal activities.

Political Consequences of Inflation

Government Stability:

Loss of Confidence:

High inflation can erode public confidence in the government and its economic policies. When people feel that the government is unable to control inflation, it can lead to political instability and changes in leadership.

Electoral Outcomes:

Inflation often becomes a key issue in elections. Incumbent governments facing high inflation rates are more likely to be voted out of office as voters seek change and stability.

Policy Responses:

Austerity Measures:

In response to high inflation, governments may implement austerity measures, including spending cuts and tax increases. While these measures can help control inflation, they often lead to public dissatisfaction and protests due to their impact on social services and welfare.

Price Controls and Subsidies:

Some governments resort to price controls and subsidies to curb inflation. While these measures can provide temporary relief, they can also lead to market distortions, shortages, and further economic problems.

Case Studies of Social and Political Consequences

Weimar Republic (Germany, 1920s):

Hyperinflation Crisis:

Post-World War I reparations and economic mismanagement led to hyperinflation in Germany. The value of the German mark plummeted, and prices soared uncontrollably.

Social Impact:

The middle class saw their savings wiped out, leading to widespread poverty and social discontent. The hyperinflation crisis contributed to a loss of faith in the Weimar government and paved the way for extremist political movements, including the rise of the Nazi Party.

Zimbabwe (2000s):

Economic Collapse:

Land reforms, economic mismanagement, and excessive money printing led to hyperinflation in Zimbabwe. At its peak, inflation reached 89.7 sextillion percent per month in November 2008.

Political Unrest:

Hyperinflation led to severe shortages of basic goods, a collapse of public services, and mass emigration. The economic crisis fueled political opposition to President Robert Mugabe's government, leading to political violence and instability.

Argentina (2000s):

Recurring Inflation:

Argentina has experienced several episodes of high inflation due to fiscal deficits, debt crises, and economic mismanagement. In the early 2000s, inflation surged following a financial crisis and currency devaluation.

Social Protests:

High inflation and economic hardship led to widespread protests and social unrest. The crisis contributed to the downfall of President Fernando de la Rúa and the subsequent economic instability.

Venezuela (2010s):

Economic Mismanagement:

Mismanagement of the economy, falling oil prices, and excessive money printing led to hyperinflation in Venezuela. The country experienced severe shortages of food, medicine, and basic necessities.

Political and Social Crisis:

The hyperinflation crisis exacerbated political divisions and led to mass protests against President Nicolás Maduro's government. The crisis has resulted in a humanitarian disaster, with millions fleeing the country and widespread poverty.

Strategies to Mitigate Social and Political Consequences

Strengthening Institutions:

Central Bank Independence:

Ensuring the independence of central banks can help maintain credible and consistent monetary policies, reducing the risk of politically driven inflationary measures.

Transparent Policies:

Transparent and predictable economic policies can help anchor inflation expectations and build public trust in government institutions.

Social Safety Nets:

Targeted Support:

Implementing social safety nets, such as unemployment benefits, food subsidies, and healthcare support, can help cushion the impact of inflation on vulnerable populations.

Progressive Taxation:

Progressive taxation policies can help redistribute wealth and reduce income inequality exacerbated by inflation.

Economic Diversification:

Reducing Dependency:

Diversifying the economy can reduce dependency on volatile sectors, such as commodities, and mitigate the impact of external shocks on inflation.

Promoting Growth:

Policies that promote sustainable economic growth, innovation, and investment can help create jobs and improve living standards, reducing the social impact of inflation.

Engaging Civil Society:

Public Dialogue:

Engaging civil society in dialogue about economic policies and inflation can help build consensus and understanding, reducing the likelihood of social unrest.

Inclusive Governance:

Inclusive governance that considers the needs and perspectives of all social groups can help address the root causes of discontent and promote social cohesion.

Conclusion

Inflation's social and political consequences are profound and far-reaching. High inflation can erode purchasing power, exacerbate income inequality, and lead to social unrest and political instability. Historical and contemporary examples demonstrate how inflation has influenced political stability and social structures in various countries.

Mitigating these consequences requires a combination of strong institutions, transparent policies, social safety nets, economic diversification, and inclusive governance. By understanding the social and political dimensions of inflation, policymakers can develop more effective strategies to promote economic stability and social well-being.

In the subsequent chapters, we will continue to explore the multifaceted nature of inflation and its broader impacts on global trade, economic growth, and social welfare, providing a comprehensive understanding of this critical economic phenomenon.

Chapter 16
The Future of Inflation Predictions and Trends

Introduction

Inflation remains a central concern for economists, policymakers, and the general public. Predicting its future trajectory involves considering a multitude of factors, from technological advancements to demographic changes and environmental challenges. This chapter delves into the potential future of global inflation, examining key trends and factors that could shape its course in the coming decades.

Key Trends Influencing Future Inflation

Technological Advancements:

Automation and Artificial Intelligence:

The rise of automation and AI has the potential to increase productivity and reduce production costs, which could exert deflationary pressures. However, these technologies might also lead to job displacement and wage stagnation for certain sectors, influencing consumer spending and inflation.

E-commerce and Digitalization:

The continued growth of e-commerce and digital platforms increases competition, leading to lower prices and improved efficiency. This trend could contribute to lower inflation rates in the retail sector.

Cryptocurrencies and Blockchain:

The adoption of cryptocurrencies and blockchain technology might alter the traditional financial system, affecting monetary policy and inflation. While still in its infancy, the impact of digital currencies on inflation remains an area of active research and debate.

Demographic Shifts:

Aging Populations:

Many developed countries are experiencing aging populations, which can slow economic growth and reduce inflationary pressures. Older populations tend to save more and spend less, leading to lower demand for goods and services.

Urbanization and Migration:

Urbanization and migration trends, especially in emerging markets, can influence inflation by altering labor markets, housing demand, and consumption patterns. Rapid urbanization can drive up prices for housing and services, contributing to localized inflationary pressures.

Environmental Factors:

Climate Change:

Climate change and environmental degradation pose significant risks to economic stability and inflation. Extreme weather events, resource scarcity, and disruptions to agricultural production can lead to supply shocks and increased prices for food and other essentials.

Transition to Green Economy:

The shift towards a green economy, involving investments in renewable energy and sustainable practices, might initially lead to higher costs and inflation. However, in the long term, sustainable practices can stabilize prices and reduce inflationary risks associated with fossil fuel dependency.

Predictions for Global Inflation

Advanced Economies:

Moderate Inflation:

Advanced economies are likely to continue experiencing moderate inflation rates, influenced by technological advancements, demographic trends, and stable monetary policies. Central banks in these regions have effective tools and frameworks to manage inflation.

Policy Challenges:

Policymakers will need to address the deflationary pressures from aging populations and technological progress while ensuring economic growth and employment.

Emerging Markets:

Higher Volatility:

Emerging markets might face more volatile inflation rates due to rapid economic growth, urbanization, and susceptibility to external shocks. These economies often have less mature monetary frameworks and are more exposed to commodity price fluctuations.

Growth and Inflation Balance:

Balancing economic growth with inflation control will be a critical challenge for emerging market policymakers. Structural reforms, improved monetary policy frameworks, and investments in human capital and infrastructure will be essential.

Technological Impact on Future Inflation

Digital Transformation:

Efficiency Gains:

Increased digitalization can lead to significant efficiency gains, reducing costs and potentially lowering inflation. For example, advancements in supply chain management and logistics can reduce production costs and retail prices.

Price Transparency:

The proliferation of online platforms enhances price transparency, allowing consumers to compare prices easily. This can limit the ability of businesses to raise prices, contributing to lower inflation.

AI and Automation:

Productivity Increases:

AI and automation can boost productivity across various sectors, leading to higher output with lower input costs. This can exert downward pressure on prices and inflation.

Wage Pressures:

However, the displacement of workers by automation could lead to wage stagnation or declines in certain sectors, reducing aggregate demand and potentially leading to deflationary pressures.

Cryptocurrencies and Financial Technology:

Monetary Policy Implications:

The rise of cryptocurrencies poses challenges for traditional monetary policy. If cryptocurrencies gain widespread adoption, central banks might find it harder to control the money supply and influence inflation.

Financial Inclusion:

Financial technology can enhance financial inclusion, allowing more people to participate in the economy. This can increase aggregate demand and potentially influence inflation dynamics.

Demographic Shifts and Their Impact on Inflation

Aging Populations:

Reduced Consumption:

As populations age, consumption patterns change, typically leading to lower overall demand for goods and services. This can reduce inflationary pressures.

Healthcare Costs:

However, aging populations can lead to increased healthcare costs, which might drive up prices in the healthcare sector and contribute to inflation in specific areas.

Urbanization and Migration:

Housing and Services:

Rapid urbanization can drive up prices for housing and services in urban areas, leading to localized inflation. Effective urban planning and infrastructure development are crucial to manage these pressures.

Labor Markets:

Migration can influence labor market dynamics, with potential impacts on wages and inflation. Inflows of labor can reduce wage pressures, while outflows can create labor shortages and drive up wages and prices.

Environmental Factors and Inflation

Climate Change:

Supply Chain Disruptions:

Extreme weather events and environmental degradation can disrupt supply chains, leading to shortages and higher prices for certain goods. This can create inflationary pressures, particularly for food and raw materials.

Resource Scarcity:

As natural resources become scarcer, prices for commodities like water, food, and energy might increase, contributing to inflation.

Green Economy Transition:

Initial Costs:

Transitioning to a green economy involves significant investments in renewable energy and sustainable practices. These initial costs might lead to higher prices for goods and services in the short term.

Long-Term Stability:

In the long term, sustainable practices can stabilize prices by reducing dependency on volatile fossil fuel markets and mitigating the economic impacts of climate change.

Conclusion

The future of global inflation will be shaped by a complex interplay of technological advancements, demographic shifts, and environmental factors. While advanced economies might experience moderate and stable inflation, emerging markets could face more volatility. Technological progress is likely to exert deflationary pressures, while demographic changes and climate-related challenges might influence inflation in various ways.

Policymakers will need to navigate these trends carefully, balancing the need for economic growth with the imperative to control inflation. Effective monetary policies, structural reforms, and investments in sustainable practices will be crucial in managing the future trajectory of inflation.

In the subsequent chapters, we will continue to explore the broader impacts of inflation on global trade, economic growth, and social welfare, providing a comprehensive understanding of this critical economic phenomenon and its implications for the future.

Chapter 17
Personal Finance and Inflation

Introduction

Inflation erodes the purchasing power of money over time, posing significant challenges for individuals trying to protect and grow their wealth. Understanding how to manage personal finances in an inflationary environment is crucial for maintaining financial stability. This chapter provides practical advice on investment strategies, savings, and overall personal finance management to help individuals safeguard their wealth against the detrimental effects of inflation.

Understanding Inflation and Its Impact

Inflation Basics:

Definition:

Inflation is the rate at which the general level of prices for goods and services rises, eroding purchasing power.

Causes:

Common causes of inflation include demand-pull inflation (excess demand), cost-push inflation (rising production costs), and built-in inflation (wage-price spirals).

Impact on Personal Finances:

Erosion of Savings:

Money saved in low-interest or non-interest-bearing accounts loses value over time as inflation reduces its purchasing power.

Rising Costs:

Everyday expenses such as groceries, housing, and healthcare increase with inflation, impacting household budgets.

Investment Returns:

Inflation affects the real return on investments. Nominal returns may appear healthy, but after adjusting for inflation, real returns can be significantly lower.

Strategies to Protect Wealth Against Inflation

1. Diversified Investment Portfolio:

Equities (Stocks):

Stocks historically offer higher returns than inflation over the long term. Investing in a diversified portfolio of equities can provide growth that outpaces inflation.

Real Estate:

Real estate is a tangible asset that typically appreciates with inflation. Rental income can also increase with inflation, providing a hedge against rising prices.

Commodities:

Investing in commodities like gold, silver, and oil can protect against inflation. These assets tend to retain value and appreciate during inflationary periods.

Inflation-Protected Securities:

Treasury Inflation-Protected Securities (TIPS) and similar instruments adjust their principal value with inflation, providing a safeguard for investors.

2. Savings and Fixed Income Strategies:

High-Yield Savings Accounts:

Opt for high-yield savings accounts that offer interest rates above the inflation rate to preserve the real value of savings.

Certificates of Deposit (CDs):

Shorter-term CDs can protect savings from inflation. Laddering CDs (staggering maturity dates) allows for better interest rate management.

Bonds:

Focus on inflation-indexed bonds, such as TIPS, which adjust for inflation and protect purchasing power.

3. Real Estate Investments:

Property Ownership:

Owning real estate, either residential or commercial, can provide a hedge against inflation. Property values and rental income often increase with inflation.

Real Estate Investment Trusts (REITs):

Investing in REITs offers exposure to real estate markets without the need for direct property ownership. REITs typically pay dividends and can appreciate in value.

4. Precious Metals and Commodities:

Gold and Silver:

These precious metals have historically been considered safe havens during inflationary periods. They retain value and can appreciate when inflation rises.

Commodity Funds:

Investing in commodity funds allows diversification into various commodities, providing a hedge against inflation-driven price increases.

5. Stock Market Investments:

Dividend-Paying Stocks:

Companies that consistently pay and increase dividends tend to be more stable and can provide income that keeps pace with inflation.

Growth Stocks:

Investing in companies with strong growth potential can result in capital appreciation that outpaces inflation.

6. Retirement Planning:

Inflation-Proof Retirement Accounts:

Consider retirement accounts that offer investment options in inflation-protected securities, equities, and real estate.

Adjust Withdrawal Rates:

Plan for inflation-adjusted withdrawals from retirement accounts to ensure sustainable income throughout retirement.

Practical Tips for Managing Personal Finances

1. Budgeting and Expense Management:

Regular Review:

Regularly review and adjust your budget to account for rising costs due to inflation. Identify areas where expenses can be reduced or optimized.

Emergency Fund:

Maintain an emergency fund that can cover 3-6 months of living expenses. Keep this fund in a high-yield savings account to mitigate the impact of inflation.

2. Debt Management:

Fixed-Rate Loans:

Opt for fixed-rate loans for mortgages, car loans, and other long-term debts. Fixed rates protect against rising interest costs due to inflation.

Pay Down High-Interest Debt:

Prioritize paying off high-interest debt, such as credit card balances, to reduce financial burden and interest expenses.

3. Income Strategies:

Side Income:

Consider generating additional income through side jobs, freelancing, or part-time work to offset inflationary pressures on your primary income.

Skill Enhancement:

Invest in education and skill development to increase your earning potential and job security in an inflationary environment.

4. Insurance and Protection:

Adjust Coverage:

Regularly review and adjust insurance coverage (health, life, property) to ensure it keeps pace with rising costs.

Index-Linked Policies:

Consider index-linked insurance policies that adjust benefits according to inflation.

5. Financial Planning:

Long-Term Goals:

Set long-term financial goals and create a comprehensive financial plan that includes strategies for inflation protection.

Professional Advice:

Consult with financial advisors to tailor investment and savings strategies to your specific needs and inflation expectations.

Conclusion

Inflation poses a significant challenge to personal finance management, but with careful planning and strategic investments, individuals can protect their wealth and maintain their purchasing power. By diversifying investments, choosing inflation-protected securities, managing expenses, and seeking professional advice, individuals can navigate inflationary environments effectively.

As we continue to explore the broader impacts of inflation in subsequent chapters, understanding how to manage personal finances in an inflationary context will provide valuable insights into maintaining financial stability and achieving long-term financial goals.

Chapter 18
Global Trade and Inflation

Introduction

Global trade and inflation are intricately linked. Trade policies, tariffs, and international trade dynamics significantly influence inflation rates across different economies. This chapter explores how international trade agreements, protectionist measures, and global trade patterns impact inflation. We delve into specific case studies and analyze the mechanisms through which trade affects prices and economic stability.

The Relationship Between Trade and Inflation

Trade and Price Levels:

Import Prices:

The cost of imported goods directly impacts the domestic price level. Lower import prices, due to free trade agreements or reductions in tariffs, can help keep inflation low.

Export Demand:

High demand for exports can drive up domestic prices, contributing to inflation. Conversely, a decline in export demand can reduce price pressures.

Exchange Rates:

Currency Valuation:

Exchange rates play a crucial role in determining the cost of imports and exports. A weaker domestic currency makes imports more expensive, contributing to inflation, while a stronger currency has the opposite effect.

Pass-Through Effect:

The extent to which exchange rate fluctuations affect domestic prices, known as the pass-through effect, varies by country and depends on factors like market structure and the degree of import dependence.

Supply Chain Dynamics:

Global Supply Chains:

Disruptions in global supply chains, such as those caused by geopolitical tensions, natural disasters, or pandemics, can lead to shortages and higher prices for goods, fueling inflation.

Production Costs:

The integration of global supply chains allows for the optimization of production costs. Changes in trade policies that disrupt these chains can increase production costs and, consequently, prices.

International Trade Agreements and Inflation

Free Trade Agreements (FTAs):

Lower Tariffs:

FTAs typically reduce or eliminate tariffs between member countries, lowering the cost of imported goods and services and exerting downward pressure on inflation.

Increased Competition:

By fostering competition, FTAs can lead to more efficient production and lower prices, further contributing to low inflation.

Regional Trade Blocs:

Economic Integration:

Regional trade blocs, such as the European Union (EU) or the North American Free Trade Agreement (NAFTA), facilitate economic integration and trade among member countries, stabilizing prices and reducing inflationary pressures.

Harmonized Policies:

Harmonized trade policies within these blocs can lead to more predictable economic environments, reducing volatility and inflation risks.

Case Study: NAFTA

Impact on Prices:

The implementation of NAFTA led to increased trade between the U.S., Canada, and Mexico. Lower tariffs resulted in reduced prices for consumer goods, helping to keep inflation in check.

Productivity Gains:

Enhanced competition and access to a larger market spurred productivity gains and innovation, contributing to stable price levels.

Protectionism and Inflation

Tariffs and Trade Barriers:

Higher Costs:

Protectionist measures, such as tariffs and quotas, increase the cost of imported goods, directly contributing to higher inflation.

Retaliation:

Retaliatory tariffs by trading partners can further escalate costs and disrupt supply chains, compounding inflationary pressures.

Trade Wars:

Economic Uncertainty:

Trade wars create economic uncertainty, impacting investment and consumer confidence. This uncertainty can lead to volatile prices and inflation.

Supply Chain Disruptions:

Trade conflicts disrupt global supply chains, leading to shortages and higher prices for goods, contributing to inflation.

Case Study: U.S.-China Trade War

Tariffs and Prices:

The U.S.-China trade war, marked by significant tariffs on a wide range of goods, led to higher costs for imported products. This contributed to inflation in sectors heavily reliant on Chinese imports.

Supply Chain Adjustments:

Companies faced increased costs as they adjusted supply chains to source goods from alternative countries, leading to higher prices for consumers.

Global Trade Dynamics and Inflation

Globalization:

Efficiency Gains:

Globalization enhances efficiency through comparative advantage and specialization, leading to lower production costs and prices, thereby reducing inflation.

Price Convergence:

Globalization promotes price convergence across countries, reducing price differentials and inflation disparities.

Decoupling and Reshoring:

Decoupling Trends:

Rising geopolitical tensions and protectionist policies have led to trends of economic decoupling, where countries seek to reduce dependence on foreign trade partners. This can lead to higher production costs and inflation.

Reshoring:

The movement of manufacturing back to domestic markets, or reshoring, can increase costs due to higher wages and production expenses, contributing to inflation.

Case Study: COVID-19 Pandemic

Supply Chain Disruptions:

The COVID-19 pandemic caused unprecedented disruptions in global supply chains, leading to shortages and higher prices for goods such as electronics, medical supplies, and consumer goods.

Inflationary Pressures:

The pandemic-induced supply chain bottlenecks resulted in significant inflationary pressures globally, as countries struggled to meet demand with constrained supply.

Mechanisms of Trade's Impact on Inflation

Direct Mechanisms:

Import Prices:

The most direct impact of trade on inflation is through import prices. Lower tariffs and improved trade relations reduce import costs, while tariffs and trade barriers increase them.

Export Demand:

Strong export demand can lead to higher domestic production and potentially higher prices if supply cannot keep pace with demand.

Indirect Mechanisms:

Exchange Rates:

Trade policies and dynamics influence exchange rates, which in turn affect import and export prices and, consequently, inflation.

Supply Chain Efficiency:

Trade policies that enhance supply chain efficiency reduce production costs and prices, whereas disruptions increase costs and inflation.

Long-Term Effects:

Investment and Innovation:

Open trade policies encourage investment and innovation, leading to productivity gains and lower long-term inflation.

Structural Changes:

Trade can lead to structural changes in economies, influencing inflation through shifts in labor markets, production processes, and consumption patterns.

Conclusion

Global trade dynamics, encompassing trade policies, international agreements, protectionist measures, and supply chain considerations, have profound effects on inflation. Understanding these relationships is crucial for policymakers and economists seeking to manage inflation effectively.

As global trade continues to evolve, the interplay between trade policies and inflation will remain a key area of focus. Future chapters will further explore the broader impacts of inflation on economic growth, social welfare, and global stability, providing a comprehensive understanding of this multifaceted economic phenomenon.

Chapter 19
Case Studies in Inflation Management

Introduction

Managing inflation is a critical task for any nation aiming to achieve economic stability and growth. Different countries have adopted various strategies to control inflation, with varying degrees of success. This chapter provides an in-depth look at how specific countries have effectively managed inflation. By examining the cases of Singapore, Switzerland, and other notable examples, we uncover the strategies that have helped these nations maintain low and stable inflation rates.

Singapore: A Model of Pragmatic Policy

Economic Context:

Open Economy:

Singapore's highly open and trade-dependent economy makes it particularly vulnerable to external price shocks.

Strong Institutions:

The country's robust legal and regulatory framework supports economic stability.

Inflation Management Strategies:

Monetary Policy:

The Monetary Authority of Singapore (MAS) uses exchange rate policy as its primary tool to manage inflation. Instead of targeting interest rates, MAS manages the Singapore dollar's value within an undisclosed policy band against a basket of currencies.

Exchange Rate Policy:

By allowing the currency to appreciate, MAS can mitigate imported inflation. Conversely, a controlled depreciation helps support export competitiveness when necessary.

Supply-Side Policies:

The government implements policies to enhance productivity and efficiency, such as investing in infrastructure, education, and technology. These efforts help contain domestic cost pressures.

Fiscal Discipline:

Singapore maintains prudent fiscal policies, avoiding excessive public debt and ensuring sustainable government spending.

Outcomes:

Low Inflation Rates:

Singapore has consistently maintained low and stable inflation rates, averaging around 2% over the past few decades.

Economic Growth:

The effective management of inflation has supported robust economic growth and high living standards.

Switzerland: Stability Through Consistency

Economic Context:

Advanced Economy:

Switzerland is known for its high-income economy, strong financial sector, and political stability.

Swiss Franc:

The Swiss franc is considered a safe-haven currency, attracting capital inflows during global uncertainties.

Inflation Management Strategies:

Monetary Policy:

The Swiss National Bank (SNB) uses a combination of interest rate policy and foreign exchange interventions to manage inflation. It sets a target range for the three-month Swiss franc LIBOR (London Interbank Offered Rate) and intervenes in the foreign exchange market when necessary.

Price Stability Goal:

The SNB's primary objective is to ensure price stability, defined as keeping inflation below 2% per year. This clear and transparent target helps anchor inflation expectations.

Strong Institutions:

Switzerland's strong institutional framework, including an independent central bank, contributes to effective inflation management.

Outcomes:

Low and Stable Inflation:

Switzerland has successfully maintained low and stable inflation, often below 2%, even during periods of global economic volatility.

Economic Resilience:

The consistent management of inflation has contributed to Switzerland's economic resilience and high standard of living.

Germany: Lessons from the Bundesbank

Economic Context:

Post-War Recovery:

Germany's post-war economic recovery was marked by efforts to rebuild and stabilize the economy.

Deutsche Mark:

The Deutsche Mark was the cornerstone of Germany's economic stability until the introduction of the euro.

Inflation Management Strategies:

Monetary Policy:

The Bundesbank, Germany's central bank, was known for its strict anti-inflationary stance. It focused on controlling the money supply and maintaining price stability.

Independence:

The Bundesbank's independence from political influence allowed it to implement policies focused solely on inflation control.

Strong Fiscal Discipline:

Germany's commitment to fiscal discipline, including balanced budgets and prudent public spending, supported monetary policy efforts.

Outcomes:

Controlled Inflation:

Germany maintained low inflation rates throughout the latter half of the 20th century, contributing to economic stability and growth.

Eurozone Influence:

The Bundesbank's success influenced the European Central Bank's (ECB) monetary policy framework, emphasizing price stability for the entire Eurozone.

Japan: Tackling Deflationary Pressures

Economic Context:

Bubble Economy:

Japan experienced a period of rapid economic growth followed by the bursting of a financial bubble in the early 1990s.

Deflation:

The country struggled with deflationary pressures for much of the subsequent decades.

Inflation Management Strategies:

Monetary Policy:

The Bank of Japan (BOJ) implemented aggressive monetary easing measures, including near-zero interest rates and quantitative easing, to combat deflation.

Abenomics:

The economic policies introduced by Prime Minister Shinzo Abe, known as Abenomics, included monetary easing, fiscal stimulus, and structural reforms aimed at reviving inflation and economic growth.

Targeting Inflation:

The BOJ set an explicit inflation target of 2% to anchor expectations and guide policy.

Outcomes:

Moderate Success:

While Japan has faced challenges in achieving its inflation target, the aggressive monetary policies have helped prevent further deflation and supported modest economic growth.

Continued Efforts:

Japan continues to innovate in its policy approaches to manage inflation and stimulate the economy.

Other Notable Examples

Australia:

Flexible Inflation Targeting:

The Reserve Bank of Australia (RBA) adopts a flexible inflation targeting framework, aiming for an inflation rate of 2-3%. This approach allows the RBA to consider economic conditions and employment levels in its policy decisions.

Success:

Australia has maintained low and stable inflation rates while supporting economic growth and resilience against global shocks.

Canada:

Inflation Control Target:

The Bank of Canada targets an inflation rate of 2%, with a control range of 1-3%. This clear and transparent target helps stabilize inflation expectations and guide monetary policy.

Coordination with Fiscal Policy:

Effective coordination between monetary and fiscal policies has helped Canada achieve stable inflation and robust economic performance.

Key Lessons in Inflation Management

Independence of Central Banks:

Central bank independence is crucial for effective inflation management. Free from political influence, central banks can implement policies focused solely on maintaining price stability.

Clear Inflation Targets:

Clear and transparent inflation targets help anchor expectations and guide policy decisions. This transparency builds credibility and trust in the central bank's commitment to controlling inflation.

Prudent Fiscal Policies:

Fiscal discipline, including balanced budgets and sustainable public spending, supports monetary policy efforts to control inflation. Governments must avoid excessive debt and spending that could fuel inflationary pressures.

Supply-Side Policies:

Enhancing productivity and efficiency through investments in infrastructure, education, and technology helps contain domestic cost pressures and support stable inflation.

Adaptability and Innovation:

Policymakers must be adaptable and innovative in their approaches to managing inflation. This includes using a range of tools and being prepared to respond to changing economic conditions.

Conclusion

The successful management of inflation requires a combination of sound monetary policy, fiscal discipline, strong institutions, and clear targets. By examining the strategies employed by countries like Singapore, Switzerland, Germany, Japan, Australia, and Canada, we gain valuable insights into the principles and practices that contribute to stable inflation and economic prosperity.

As we conclude this chapter, we recognize that while the specific strategies may vary, the underlying principles of prudent policy, institutional strength, and adaptability are universally applicable. The next and final chapter will synthesize the insights gained from our exploration of inflation and its global impact, offering a comprehensive understanding of this critical economic phenomenon and its implications for the future.

Chapter 20
Navigating the Inflation Tide
A Global Call to Action

Introduction

As we reach the conclusion of our exploration into the complex world of inflation, it becomes clear that managing inflation is a multifaceted challenge requiring a comprehensive, coordinated approach. Drawing from the insights of previous chapters, this chapter proposes a holistic strategy to navigate the inflation tide. We call for global cooperation, innovative policies, and a proactive stance to address inflation effectively, ensuring economic stability and prosperity for all nations.

Synthesis of Key Insights

Understanding the Origins and Mechanics:

Economic Fundamentals:

Inflation is deeply rooted in economic fundamentals, including money supply, demand, and production costs. Effective management requires a thorough understanding of these principles.

Historical Lessons:

Historical episodes of hyperinflation, such as those in the Weimar Republic and Zimbabwe, highlight the devastating effects of uncontrolled inflation and underscore the importance of sound monetary policy.

Central Banks and Monetary Policy:

Central Bank Independence:

The independence of central banks is crucial for maintaining credibility and implementing effective anti-inflationary measures without political interference.

Monetary Policy Tools:

Central banks have a range of tools at their disposal, including interest rates, reserve requirements, and open market operations. These tools must be used judiciously to control inflation without stifling growth.

Global Trade and Supply Chains:

Trade Dynamics:

International trade agreements and policies significantly impact inflation through import prices and supply chain efficiencies. Protectionist measures can exacerbate inflation by increasing costs.

Supply Chain Resilience:

Disruptions in global supply chains, as seen during the COVID-19 pandemic, can lead to inflationary pressures. Building resilient and diversified supply chains is essential for economic stability.

Technological Advancements:

Innovation and Productivity:

Technological advancements can enhance productivity and reduce costs, helping to mitigate inflationary pressures. However, they also require adaptive policies to manage transitional impacts on the labor market.

Fiscal Policies and Debt Management:

Fiscal Discipline:

Prudent fiscal policies, including sustainable government spending and debt management, are vital for preventing inflation. Excessive debt can lead to inflationary pressures and economic instability.

Coordinated Efforts:

Effective coordination between monetary and fiscal policies enhances their combined impact on controlling inflation and supporting growth.

A Global Call to Action

To navigate the inflation tide effectively, we propose a comprehensive approach centered on global cooperation, innovative policies, and proactive measures. This global call to action outlines key strategies for policymakers, central banks, international organizations, and other stakeholders.

1. Strengthening International Cooperation:

Global Frameworks:

Develop and strengthen international frameworks for economic cooperation and policy coordination. Institutions like the International Monetary Fund (IMF) and the World Bank can play pivotal roles in fostering collaboration.

Trade Agreements:

Promote and enhance international trade agreements that reduce tariffs, eliminate trade barriers, and facilitate smoother global supply chains. Cooperation on trade policies can help stabilize prices and mitigate inflation.

2. Enhancing Central Bank Policies:

Clear Communication:

Central banks should maintain clear and transparent communication regarding their inflation targets and policy actions. This helps anchor expectations and build public trust.

Adaptive Strategies:

Central banks must remain flexible and adaptive, ready to adjust policies in response to changing economic conditions and emerging challenges.

3. Innovating Fiscal Policies:

Sustainable Spending:

Governments should prioritize sustainable spending practices, avoiding excessive debt accumulation that can fuel inflation. Investments in infrastructure, education, and technology should be balanced with fiscal discipline.

Targeted Interventions:

Implement targeted fiscal interventions to support vulnerable populations during inflationary periods. Social safety nets and subsidies for essential goods can help mitigate the impact on low-income households.

4. Building Resilient Supply Chains:

Diversification:

Encourage diversification of supply sources to reduce dependence on any single region or country. This enhances resilience against disruptions and helps stabilize prices.

Technological Integration:

Leverage technology to enhance supply chain efficiency and transparency. Innovations like blockchain and AI can improve tracking, reduce bottlenecks, and optimize logistics.

5. Embracing Technological Advancements:

Productivity Gains:

Invest in technology and innovation to drive productivity gains and reduce production costs. This can help mitigate inflationary pressures in the long run.

Workforce Adaptation:

Implement policies to support workforce adaptation to technological changes, including retraining and upskilling programs. This ensures that the benefits of technological advancements are widely shared.

6. Fostering Sustainable Development:

Climate Policies:

Integrate climate change considerations into economic policies. Sustainable development practices can reduce the risk of climate-induced supply disruptions and their inflationary impacts.

Green Investments:

Promote investments in renewable energy and sustainable practices to reduce reliance on volatile energy markets and mitigate inflation driven by energy prices.

Proactive Stance for Future Challenges

Anticipating Future Trends:

Demographic Shifts:

Prepare for demographic changes, such as aging populations and migration patterns, which can influence inflation dynamics. Policies should address the economic impacts of these shifts.

Geopolitical Risks:

Stay vigilant to geopolitical risks that can disrupt global trade and supply chains. Proactive diplomacy and international cooperation are key to mitigating these risks.

Data-Driven Decision Making:

Advanced Analytics:

Utilize advanced data analytics and economic modeling to inform policy decisions. Real-time data and predictive analytics can enhance the accuracy and effectiveness of inflation management strategies.

Monitoring Indicators:

Continuously monitor a range of economic indicators, including price levels, wage growth, and supply chain performance, to detect early signs of inflationary pressures.

Conclusion

Navigating the inflation tide requires a concerted global effort, combining sound monetary and fiscal policies, technological innovation, and international cooperation. By learning from past experiences and adopting a proactive, forward-looking approach, we can effectively manage inflation and ensure economic stability and prosperity.

As we conclude this comprehensive exploration of inflation, it is evident that while the challenges are significant, the opportunities for effective management and positive outcomes are equally substantial. A global call to action, underpinned by collaboration, innovation, and resilience, offers the best path forward in addressing the complexities of inflation in an interconnected world.

THE END!

www.ingramcontent.com/pod-product-compliance
Lightning Source LLC
Chambersburg PA
CBHW071458220526
45472CB00003B/843